Wayside Wildflowers
of the
Pacific Northwest

photography and text by
Dr. Dee Strickler

illustration and graphic design by
Zoe Strickler

PACIFIC RHODODENDRON
Rhododendron macrophylum

Note: For a description see page 125.

Dedication

Dedicated to
CLAIRE
I couldn't make a fisherwoman of her,
so she made a flower lover of me.

Library of Congress Catalog Card Number: 92-76062
ISBN 1-56044-185-2

Published by The Flower Press
Columbia Falls, Montana

Publishing Consultant:
SkyHouse Publishers, an imprint of
Falcon Press Publishing Co., Inc.,
Helena and Billings, Montana

To order extra copies of this book, contact:
The Flower Press, 192 Larch Lane, Columbia Falls, MT 59912, or
Falcon Press, P.O. Box 1718, Helena MT 59624,
or call toll-free 1-800-582-2665.

Second printing 1996
Printed in Hong Kong

Acknowledgements

In the preparation of a book of this scope, many people provide invaluable assistance, such as the identification of difficult species, picture selection, editing and proofreading. I gratefully extend my thanks and appreciation for species identification to Joy Mastrogiuseppe, curator of the herbarium, Washington State University; Veva Stansell, plant specialist, USDA Forest Service, Gold Beach, Oregon; Professor Kenton Chambers, Botany Department, Oregon State University; Jennifer Dimling, Forest Botanist, USDA Forest Service, Eugene, Oregon; Mark Egger, University of Washington; Peter Stickney, USDA Forest Service, Missoula, Montana and Peter Lesica, rare plant specialist, Missoula. Special thanks go to Dr. Jeanette Oliver, biologist, Flathead Valley Community College, for much generous help.

My daughter, Zoe Strickler, contributed greatly with the overall graphic format, with drawings and consultation on artwork, but the Visual Guide layout and drawings were the responsibility of the author.

My son, Jack, supplied the photo of rabbitbrush, p 78.

Recognition is also due Skyhouse Publishers and Falcon Graphics, Helena, Montana, for the expert cropping of pictures, color application to the Visual Guide and for management of the printing.

My wife, Claire, also deserves special recognition for invaluable help with photo selection, editing, proofreading and back cover photo, and for her constant support and encouragement.

—Whitefish, Montana. December 1992.

About the author

Dee Strickler is a wood scientist and technologist holding a B.S. from Washington State University, an M.S. from Syracuse University and a doctorate from Duke University. His forestry undergraduate curriculum included a minor in botany. As wood technologist on the College of Engineering faculty of Washington State University for many years, he authored over 50 technical publications and reports on original research in the fields of wood properties and glued wood products.

Dr. Strickler has enjoyed wildflower photography for more than 20 years and herein shares that interest and enjoyment with others.

Contents

Contents

Introduction

The photographs in this book show nearly 400 species of wildflowers, mostly the more common plants found growing along the roads and highways, trails and byways of the Pacific Northwest. In addition, some uncommon or rare flowers that I chanced upon in my travels find a place here. The species are arranged alphabetically by families. In my pictures I strive to capture natural colors and the features most noticeable to the casual observer, as well as details that may require more than a casual glance to appreciate.

A commentary accompanies each photograph, describing the most noticeable features of the blossoms, plants and leaves. Also described are the blooming period, habitat and growing ranges of the species pictured. Pertinent comments and interesting facets also accompany the descriptions of many species.

The photos show leaves and stems when it is possible to do so without losing detail and brightness of the flowers. The pictures therefore emphasize primarily the flowers, but I made a conscious effort to include other details that enhance the beauty of plants and aid in identification of species.

Discussions in this book minimize the technical jargon that botanists must employ for precise description of plant and flower structure. The book is intended for all lovers of nature, including the specialist. Hikers, outdoorsmen, travellers, students and amateur botanists will find it helpful, I hope, as a field guide to the fullest enjoyment of our natural heritage.

Unfortunately, a book of this scope cannot include every species that one may find in the Northwest. I tried to show representative species of all the major genera, but even that is not possible in the largest plant families. The sunflower family *(Asteraceae)* for example, contains approximately 1000 species in 100 genera in the Northwest. Inclusion of just one species from each genus in this family would therefore require an inordinate amount of space. Many less showy species, weeds, common agricultural escapes and introduced pests, such as dandelions, also do not merit a place in this book. Although native plants receive preferential treatment, a few exceptions of showy, alien flowers, such as scotch broom, are included. The author hopes he has achieved a fair balance and that everyone can enjoy *Wayside Wildflowers of the Pacific Northwest.*

The author has previously published three books on the showy wildflowers of the northern Rocky Mountain states, namely *Prairie Wildflowers, Forest Wildflowers* and *Alpine Wildflowers.* Because the region of this book overlaps part of the area covered in that series, I have already published a good many of the species shown here. Within any given genus, however, I made a conscious effort to show different species from the earlier works. In addition, most of the pictures in this book are new since the prior publications.

Floral Areas of the Northwest

For the purposes of this book the Pacific Northwest is defined as the states of Washington, Oregon, Idaho and western Montana, as well as adjacent southwestern Canada. Within this region one finds a bewildering diversity of habitats for plants and a vast array of wildflowers. For its size the Pacific Northwest probably contains the greatest variety of plant species of any comparable region in North America and certainly one of the most diverse florae of any comparable area of the world outside the tropics.

The following paragraphs describe the general life zones of the region:

Coastal Beaches and Pacific Rim. Along the coast of Oregon, Washington and British Columbia, the prevailing winds blow off the ocean. Cool, wet weather generally prevails, including measurable amounts of moisture in the form of condensed fog. Some plants have adapted to the environment of sandy beaches, such as beach strawberry and beach pea. They serve the valuable function of helping to retard beach erosion and sand dune formation and movement. Many more species thrive in the coastal scrub and conifer forests behind the beaches.

Coast Range. Running north to south from coastal British Columbia into California, including the Olympic Peninsula, the coast range of mountains generally reaches 20 to 30 miles in width. From sea level to mountain tops it features dense forests of mixed conifers. Moisture laden winds off the ocean must rise to pass over these coastal mountains. In doing so, they cool and lose considerable moisture, mostly as rain. On the Olympic Peninsula the mountains attain greater heights than those farther south, giving rise to rain forests that receive more than 100 inches of precipitation yearly. The east slopes of the Coast Range are somewhat drier than the west side, because the winds tend to warm as they descend the leeward side.

The forest overstory of the coastal mountains shades out many species of flowering plants, but others thrive in the forest habitat. Serpentine rock formations, fire and human activities create forest openings and meadows that also foster flowering plant growth.

In the Siskiyou mountains of southwestern Oregon, distinct differences in the flora occur. Here one finds many species not encountered farther north. This flora begins the transition to that of northern California Coast and Sierra ranges.

Puget Trough and Williamette Valley. In the shadow of the coastal mountains the valleys receive less rainfall, but generally mild weather patterns prevail. Sufficient moisture falls to nurture forests of mixed conifers and some hardwoods. Many of the same species of wildflowers occur in the valleys as in the Coast Range, but other new and different species also appear.

The Cascades. Considerably higher than the Coast Range, the Cascades again cause the westerly winds to rise. The western slope receives copious rainfall and the east slope decreasing amounts. The flora of the west slope resembles that of the valleys and Coast Range, but one can also find many different species here. On the drier east slope, ponderosa pine, lodgepole pine and scrub oak forests replace Douglas fir and western hemlock. Here a rich flora shows the influence of both western forests and the drier lands farther east.

Columbia Basin and Great Basin. In the plateau and canyon country east of the Cascades, moisture in the form of rain and snow varies from as little as 6 inches to around 20 inches per year. This region stretches across central and southeastern Oregon and southern Idaho and northward across central and eastern Washington into south-central British Columbia. It includes the northern portion of the Great Basin of Nevada and Utah, which has no drainage to the ocean. This vast area can be further divided into several separate life zones depending upon rainfall and elevation, from desert or near desert to the lush Palouse hills of eastern Washington. The area generally features bunch grass slopes and sagebrush prairies. Despite the dry, barren aspect much of the year, many wildflowers adapt readily to this habitat and flourish, especially in spring. Here one finds the balsamroots and numerous species of biscuitroot and locoweeds among many others.

Blue Mountains. East of the sagebrush flats and canyons, the Blue Mountains rear up in central and northeastern Oregon and southeastern Washington. The many wildflowers here generally comprise a mixture of east slope Cascades, Great and Columbia Basins and Rocky Mountain floras. Bunchgrass on the foothills gives way to ponderosa pine and eventually to Douglas fir, true firs and spruce at the higher elevations.

Rocky Mountains. The Rockies form another barrier to westerly winds and precipitation increases again over the mountains. Mixed conifer forests on the mountains intersperse with meadows and open slopes in the valleys and canyons. Northern Idaho and northwestern Montana often feel the influence of intermittent weather patterns from the gulf of Alaska and central British Columbia. Higher rainfall in this area allows some plants to grow that typify the coastal forests and Cascades. However, one also finds a distinct flora here that shows some influence of prairie plants from the Great Plains to the east, especially in the intermontane valleys.

Alpine and Subalpine. Finally a marked change in plant species occurs at elevations above the dense coniferous forests. Alpine is usually defined as the treeless region above timberline. A poorly marked subalpine zone, composed of smaller or stunted trees intermixed with meadows, rocky open slopes and brushy areas, provides a transition from dense montane forests into alpine habitat. Some wildflower species can adapt to more than one of these zones, while others exist only in one specific niche.

Alpine terrain occurs at higher elevations in the Olympics, Cascades and Rockies, including the Wallowa mountains of northeastern Oregon. In general, wildflower species vary much less among the different alpine areas than among comparable areas at lower elevations. In addition, subalpine plants flourish on top of some mountains that are not high enough to develop true alpine flora, such as the Blue Mountains and Wenatchee Mountains of Washington.

Alpine species commonly grow low to the ground as a defense against strong winds and blowing snow and ice crystals on mountain tops and exposed ridges. Many of them form dense, compact, ground-covering mats or cushions. Most of them are perennials, because the short alpine growing season does not allow enough time for them to complete their life cycles in one brief season. Many alpine flowers display brilliant colors and commonly develop full-sized blossoms on dwarfed plants. Some of our most glorious floral displays occur in the high alpine reaches where human visitors happen by only rarely.

Visual Guide to Families and Genera

To aid the amateur in the identification of Northwest wildflowers, pages 10 to 19 contain a visual-graphic guide to the flowers pictured in this book. In addition, pages 262 to 263 present glossaries of the technical terms deemed necessary by the author.

In order to use the visual guide effectively in the field, one must note a few characteristics of a flower unknown to the observer. Note first whether the plant is an herb (dies back to the ground each year without a woody stem), a shrub or small tree with a woody stem at the base, or a vine. Then observe the petals or showy sepals if petals are not present. If the petals or sepals occur in 3's or 6's and if the leaf veins are parallel instead of netted, the plant is a monocot (has just one cotyledon or section of the seed) and appears near the front of the book and of the guide. If the petals occur in 4's, 5's or more than 6's and the leaf veins make netted patterns, the plant is a dicot (two cotyledons). A note of caution is needed here, because exceptions frequently occur in nature and one should study several flowers, if possible, before referring to a given section of the guide. One version of Murphy's law holds that one will invariably find an exception to the rules when trying to identify an unknown flower.

Further divisions of the guide separate families or genera depending upon whether the flower in question is regular (symmetrical and can be divided in half in more than one plane to produce two mirror images) or if it is irregular and can only be divided in one plane to produce two mirror images. Then one needs to notice if the flowers are solitary or very few on the stem or numerous on each stem. One section of the guide also shows unusual or odd flower shapes and another section has special types of inflorescences.

If all else fails, simply leaf through the guide and try to match the flower in question to one in the guide. The guide also shows a range of colors commonly found in the various genera, although color affords a poor basis for wildflower identification. In particular, species that usually bear blue, purple or red flowers will frequently produce white sports or albinos. Likewise normally white flowers will sometimes display colored specimens, usually pink or pale blue. Yellow-flowered species, on the other hand, seldom exhibit another color.

HERBS
Flower Parts in 3's and 6's (Monocots)
(Leaves mostly smooth, entire and parallel veined.)

Regular Flowers

Solitary Blossom or Few Per Stem

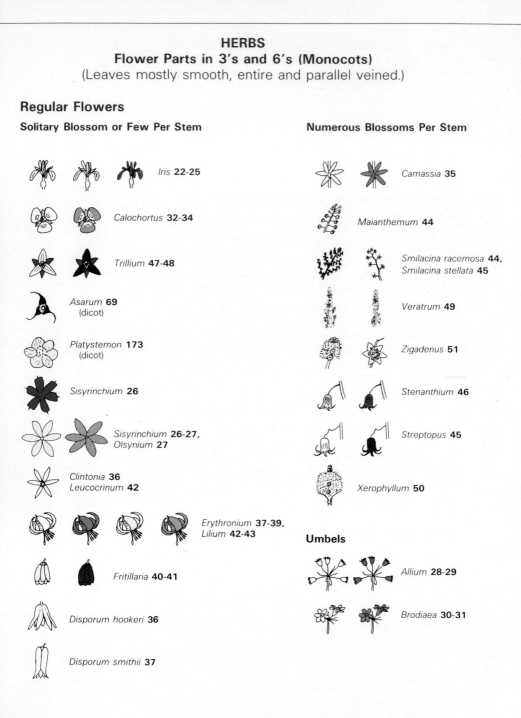

Iris **22-25**

Calochortus **32-34**

Trillium **47-48**

Asarum **69**
(dicot)

Platystemon **173**
(dicot)

Sisyrinchium **26**

Sisyrinchium **26-27**,
Olsynium **27**

Clintonia **36**
Leucocrinum **42**

Erythronium **37-39**,
Lilium **42-43**

Fritillaria **40-41**

Disporum hookeri **36**

Disporum smithii **37**

Numerous Blossoms Per Stem

Camassia **35**

Maianthemum **44**

Smilacina racemosa **44**,
Smilacina stellata **45**

Veratrum **49**

Zigadenus **51**

Stenanthium **46**

Streptopus **45**

Xerophyllum **50**

Umbels

Allium **28-29**

Brodiaea **30-31**

HERBS
Flower Parts in 3's and 6's (Monocots)
(Leaves mostly smooth, entire and parallel veined)

Irregular Flowers (Orchids)

With Green Leaves

  Calypso bulbosa **52**

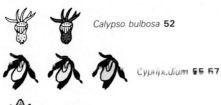 *Cypripedium* **55 57**

 Epipactis gigantea **58**

 Habenaria **57-59**

 Habenaria viridis **59**

 Orchis rotundifolia **60**

Without Green Leaves

Coralorhiza maculata **53**

Coralorhiza mertensiana **53**

Coralorhiza striata **54**

Eburophyton austinae **54**

HERBS
Flower Parts in 4's and 5's (Dicots)
(Leaves variable, mostly net veined)

Regular Flowers

Flower Parts in 4's
Solitary Blossom or Few Per Stem

 Cornus canadensis 111

  Camissonia 165, 168, Oenothera 168

 Eschscholzia 172, Papaver 173

 Clematis hirsutissima 199

Numerous Blossoms Per Stem

 Brassicaceae 97-99

 Clarkia pulchella 165

 Clarkia 164

 Epilobium 166-167

 Oenothera 167-168

 Frasera 143

 Digitalis 234

 Hypopitys 119

 Cleome lutea 103

Flower Parts in 5's
Solitary Blossom or Few per Stem

 Monotropa uniflora 121

 Pyrola uniflora 124

 Anemone 193-194, Oxalis 171, Arenaria Potentilla 216

 Trollius 204, Ranunculus 202-203

 Paeonia 205

 Darlingtonia 224

 Parnassia fimbriata 227

 Saxifraga oppositifolia 229

 Silene acaulis 109

Phlox 176-177, Douglasia 190-191

 Campanula 101-102

Hesperochiron 149

Gentiana 144

 Calandrinia 182

Convolvulus 110

Regular Flowers
Multiple Blossoms Per Stem

Flower Parts (Petals) Free

 Arenaria **108**, *Claytonia* **183**, *Linum* **159**

 Anemone **193**, *Ranunculus* **203**

 Fragaria **212**, *Potentilla* **216**

 Luetkea **214**

 Mentzelia **160**

 Geranium **146**

 Hypericum **153**

Iliamna **162**, *Sidalcea* **161-163** *Sphaeralcea* **161**

Saxifraga **227-228**, *Suksdorfia* **228-230**

Lithophragma **225**

 Mitella **226**

 Pyrola **122-123**

Sedum **113**

Sarcodes sanguinea **127**

Flower Parts (Petals) Fused

 Androsache **187**, *Apocynum* **68**, *Boraginaceae* **92-96**

 Mertensia **95**

 Campanula **101-102**

 Collomia **174**, *Ipomopsis* **175**

 Phlox **176-177**, *Phacelia* **152**, *Nemophila* **151**

 Phlox speciosa **177**

 Polemonium **178**

Geum **212**

Tiarella **231**

Tellima **230**

Pterospora **122**

Gentiana sceptrum **144**

 Asclepias **69**

HERBS
Flower Parts in 7's or More

Regular Flowers

 *Opuntia* **100**

 Trientalis **191**

 Nuphar **163**

 *Lewisia rediviva* **184-185**

Lewisia pygmaea **184-186**, *Caltha* **195**, *Dryas* **210**, *Anemone* **193**

Irregular Flowers

Flower Parts in 4's

 Veronica **256**

 Prunella **155**

 Stachys **158**

 Scutellaria **156**

 Collinsia **234**

 Clarkia rhomboidea **166**

 *Pedicularis* **241-243**

 *Pedicularis* **242-246**

Orthocarpus **240**, *Triphysaria* **240**

 Castilleja **232-233**

Flower Parts in 5's

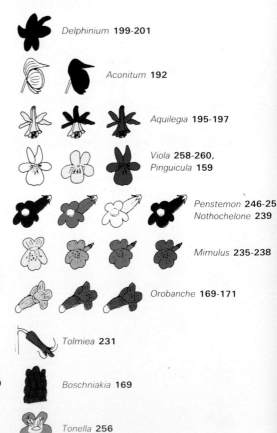 *Delphinium* **199-201**

Aconitum **192**

Aquilegia **195-197**

Viola **258-260**, *Pinguicula* **159**

Penstemon **246-25**, *Nothochelone* **239**

Mimulus **235-238**

Orobanche **169-171**

Tolmiea **231**

Boschniakia **169**

Tonella **256**

HERBS

Odd Flower Shapes

Dodecatheon **188-189**

Vancouveria **92**

Dicentra **141-142**

Rhinanthus **253**

Corydalis **141**

Thalictrum **203**

Eriophorum **61**

Allotropa **115**

Darlingtonia **224**

Pedicularis groenlandica **244**

Pea Flowers (Legumes)

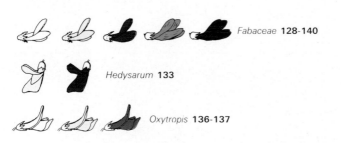

Fabaceae **128-140**

Hedysarum **133**

Oxytropis **136-137**

HERBS
Special Inflorescences
Composite Heads *(Asteraceae)* 70-89

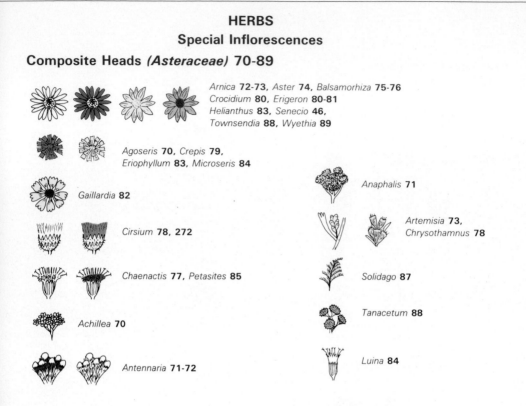

Arnica **72-73**, Aster **74**, Balsamorhiza **75-76**
Crocidium **80**, Erigeron **80-81**
Helianthus **83**, Senecio **46**,
Townsendia **88**, Wyethia **89**

Agoseris **70**, Crepis **79**,
Eriophyllum **83**, Microseris **84**

Gaillardia **82**

Cirsium **78, 272**

Chaenactis **77**, Petasites **85**

Achillea **70**

Antennaria **71-72**

Anaphalis **71**

Artemisia **73**,
Chrysothamnus **78**

Solidago **87**

Tanacetum **88**

Luina **84**

Umbels

Apiaceae **62-68**,
Angelica **62-63**, Glehnia **64**,
Heracleum **64**,
Lomatium **64-67**

Eriogonum **179-180**

Spraguea **187**

Isopyrum **201**

Allium **28-29**,
Brodiaea **30-31**

Asclepias **69**

 Douglasia **190**

HERBS
Special Inflorescences (continued)
Tight Clusters of Tiny Flowers

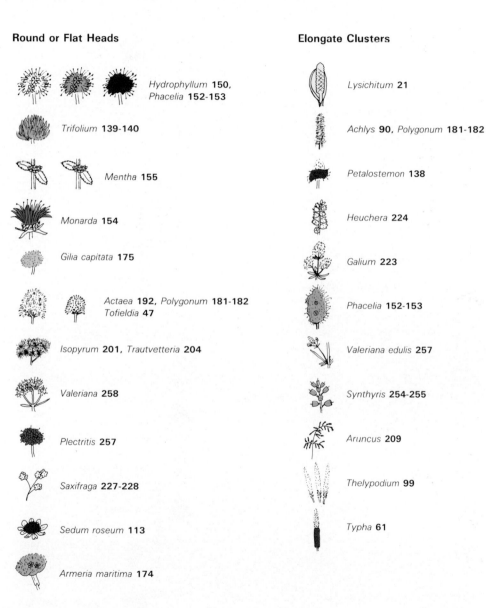

Round or Flat Heads

Hydrophyllum **150,**
Phacelia **152-153**

Trifolium **139-140**

Mentha **155**

Monarda **154**

Gilia capitata **175**

Actaea **192,** *Polygonum* **181-182**
Tofieldia **47**

Isopyrum **201,** *Trautvetteria* **204**

Valeriana **258**

Plectritis **257**

Saxifraga **227-228**

Sedum roseum **113**

Armeria maritima **174**

Elongate Clusters

Lysichitum **21**

Achlys **90,** *Polygonum* **181-182**

Petalostemon **138**

Heuchera **224**

Galium **223**

Phacelia **152-153**

Valeriana edulis **257**

Synthyris **254-255**

Aruncus **209**

Thelypodium **99**

Typha **61**

SHRUBS AND SMALL TREES
Flower Parts (Petals) Free

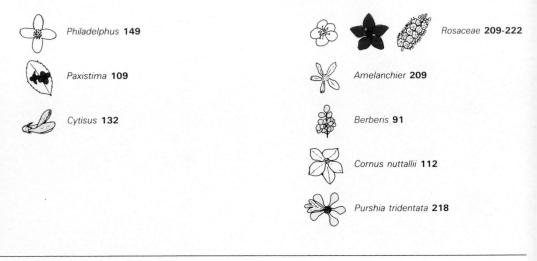

Parts in 4's

Philadelphus **149**

Paxistima **109**

Cytisus **132**

Parts in 5's

Rosaceae **209-222**

Amelanchier **209**

Berberis **91**

Cornus nuttallii **112**

Purshia tridentata **218**

Flower Parts (Petals) Fused

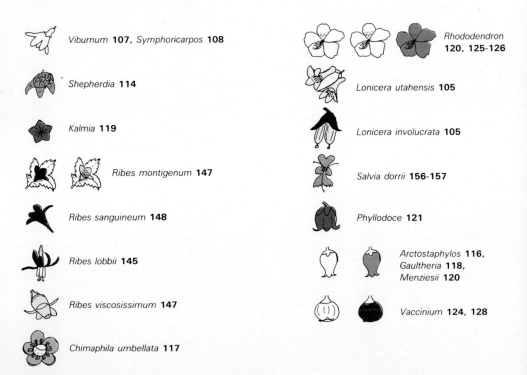

Viburnum **107**, Symphoricarpos **108**

Shepherdia **114**

Kalmia **119**

Ribes montigenum **147**

Ribes sanguineum **148**

Ribes lobbii **145**

Ribes viscosissimum **147**

Chimaphila umbellata **117**

Rhododendron **120, 125-126**

Lonicera utahensis **105**

Lonicera involucrata **105**

Salvia dorrii **156-157**

Phyllodoce **121**

Arctostaphylos **116**, Gaultheria **118**, Menziesii **120**

Vaccinium **124, 128**

SHRUBS AND SMALL TREES

Tight Clusters of Tiny Flowers

 Cornus stolonifera **111,**
Sorbus **221,** *Spiraea* **222**

  Ceanothus **206,**
Sambucus racemosa **106**

 Holodiscus **213**

 Oplopanax **68**

 Prunus virginiana **217**

 *Spiraea* **221, 222**

Umbels

 Rhamnus purshiana **208**

 Viburnum **107**

VINES

 Linnaea borealis **103**

 Lonicera ciliosa **104**

 Arctostaphylos uva-ursi **117**

 Clematis columbiana **198**

 Clematis ligusticifolia **198**

 Convolvulus **110**

 Marah **114**

 Ceanothus prostratus **207**

 Rubus **221**

 Asarum caudatum **69**

 Rhus **62**

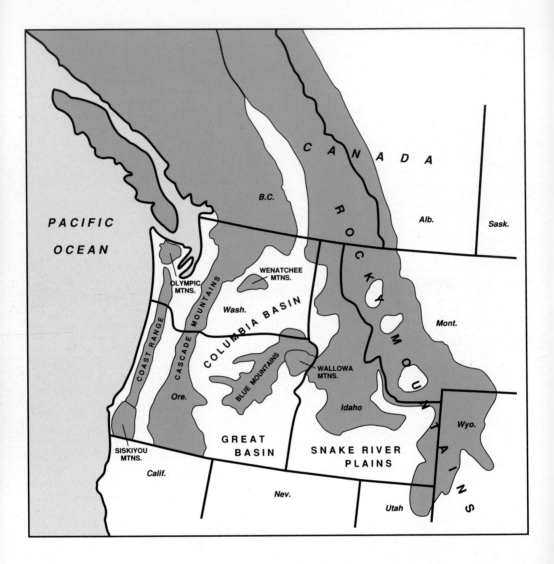

Arum or Calla Lily Family *(Araceae)*

YELLOW SKUNK CABBAGE

Lysichitum americanum. Very early in the spring a yellow hood, called a spathe, pushes through the mud of swampy ground and opens to reveal a fleshy, upright stalk about 4 to 8 inches high that is covered with tiny, greenish yellow flowers. Numerous smooth, oval leaves soon follow and rise from the fleshy root. The leaves generally reach 2 to 3 feet long or longer at maturity and 1 foot wide, the largest leaves of all native plants in the Northwest. Although skunk cabbage is a monocot, the leaves have netted veins, contrary to the rule of parallel veins for monocots. HABITAT: Skunk cabbage haunts wet woods and bogs at the lower elevations. RANGE: Alaska to W Montana and south through the Cascades and Coast Range to central California. COMMENT: Wild animals, especially bears and elk, feed on skunk cabbage in spring. All parts of the plant are edible, but for human consumption, they should be boiled or dried to reduce the concentration of oxalic acid, which otherwise produces a bitter taste.

Iris Family *(Iridaceae)*

SISKIYOU IRIS

Iris bracteata. Siskiyou iris normally produces two blossoms per stem. The white or pale yellow petals and sepals display gorgeous yellow throats with purple or brownish veins. Beneath each flower, two leaflike bracts enfold the ovary and its supporting pedicel. Above, a floral tube connects the ovary to the upper flower parts. In this species the pedicel rises 2 to 3 inches and the tube is very short—about 1/4 inch. Floral stems of Siskiyou iris reach 8 to 12 inches high, and narrow basal leaves are somewhat longer. It blooms in May and June. HABITAT: Openings in woods and mountains. RANGE: Southwestern Oregon and N California.

Iris Family *(Iridaceae)*

SLENDER TUBED IRIS

Iris chrysophylla. In this delicate little *Iris*, the pedicel supporting the ovary is very short and the tube above the ovary stretches 2 to 4 inches. The extreme length of the tube readily identifies this species. Dark veins mark the cream, yellow- or blue-tinged petals. Two leafy bracts, unequal in length, enfold the ovary and most of the floral tube. Two or three short stem leaves clasp the stem and grassy basal leaves grow up to 16 inches long. The plants spread by rhizomes underground and often form tight clumps. Blooming occurs from March to June. HABITAT: Valleys into the mountains. RANGE: Western Oregon and NW California.

Iris Family *(Iridaceae)*

DOUGLAS' IRIS

Iris douglasiana. All *Iris* spread by underground rhizomes, and this one forms clumps that are decumbent or reclining at the base. The flower stalks rise 6 to 20 inches or more and may branch once or twice. Purple or lavender or sometimes cream-colored flowers crown the stems and normally show some lighter shades in the throat. In this species the pedicel and tube vary but usually reach about the same length. The leaves are 1/3 to 3/4 inch wide, 12 to 28 inches long and pink or reddish at the base. A few shorter leaves clasp the stem. This one blooms in spring. HABITAT: Sandy coastal meadows and open slopes. RANGE: Southwestern Oregon into California. COMMENT: Douglas' iris hybridizes rather freely with both golden and Oregon iris.

Iris Family *(Iridaceae)* [Golden Color Phase]

GOLDEN IRIS

Iris innominata. Golden iris normally opens bright yellow flowers, but occasional blue or purple blossoms probably indicate hybridization with Douglas' or Oregon iris. Reddish brown veins tint the petals, especially in the throat. They spread 3 to 4 inches across. The tube, connecting the ovary to the upper floral parts, reaches about 1 inch in length and the pedicel below the ovary is very short. This iris grows 1/2 to 2 feet tall. Blooming occurs in late spring. HABITAT: Moist forest openings and roadsides. RANGE: The Siskiyou mountains of SW Oregon and N California. COMMENT: No less than four species of white or yellow *Iris* reside in SW Oregon and range into California.

Iris Family *(Iridaceae)* [Blue Color Phase]

Iris Family *(Iridaceae)*

OREGON IRIS, TOUGHLEAF IRIS

Iris tenax. This iris varies from white to yellow to blue or purple, but lavender shades predominate. Darker guide lines usually beautify the petals over a yellow basal area. The flower stems normally reach about 1 foot high and slender grass-like leaves reach a little higher. A couple of short leaves attach on the stem, and two leafy bracts arise at noticeably different levels below the ovary. April to June for this one.
HABITAT: Open areas and roadsides to moderate elevations. RANGE: West slope of the Cascades to the coast, SW Washington to NW California.
COMMENT: Native Americans made ropes from the tough, fibrous leaves of this plant.

Iris Family *(Iridaceae)*

Iris Family *(Iridaceae)*

BLUE-EYED GRASS

Sisyrinchium angustifolium. In the Northwest we have four poorly differentiated varieties of blue-eyed grass. All but one have unbranched stems, 6 to 14 inches tall, with leaves originating from the plant base. However, two sharp-pointed, leaf-like bracts subtend the flowers, which may occur singly or up to five or more in an umbel. The bracts may or may not project above the flowers. Grass-like, sharp-pointed leaves usually grow shorter than the flower stems. Six oblong or elliptic tepals radiate from a short floral tube; the color varies from pale to dark blue or bluish purple, with yellow anthers and a yellow center eye. Blooms can appear from April to July. HABITAT: Usually grassy meadows. RANGE: Alaska to Canada and south to Baja and New Mexico. COMMENT: If a member of the iris or lily families appears to have six uniform petals, they will in reality be three petals and three sepals, collectively called "tepals."

YELLOW-EYED GRASS

Sisyrinchium californicum. One yellow species of *Sisyrinchium* also graces the Pacific Northwest. In form, the plants closely resemble the blue-eyed species. The grass-like leaves, from 2 to 10 inches tall, assume a dull green shade. The stems stand somewhat taller and grow quite flat, commonly tapering to thin wings on the edges. Two leafy bracts subtend the flowers and usually reach different lengths. Brownish veins accent the lemon yellow to deep yellow tepals. The two to seven flowers usually bloom one at a time in late spring and early summer and only last for one day, often fading by afternoon. HABITAT: Wet ground behind coastal sand dunes to lake shores at low elevations. RANGE: Southern Vancouver Island to S California, entirely west of the Cascades.

Iris Family *(Iridaceae)*

GRASS WIDOW

Olsynium douglasii. (Sisyrinchium douglasii.) Grass widows spread six delicate tepals, usually lavender, but sometimes magenta or albino, about 1 inch in diameter. The plant normally displays two blossoms on a smooth stem, 6 to 10 inches high. Two short, grass-like leaves sheath the stem at the base and two bracts of considerably different length subtend the flowers and reach above them. Blooming occurs early in the spring, soon after snow melt. HABITAT: Grassy slopes and flats at low elevation to open pine forest into the mountains. RANGE: Vancouver Island to California, west of the Cascades; the Columbia Gorge and adjacent eastern slopes of the Cascades. COMMENT: Very similar, *O. inflatum* shows a much more inflated pistil and ranges east of the Cascades from S British Columbia to Idaho and south to Utah and California.

Lily Family *(Liliaceae)*

Lily Family *(Liliaceae)*

NODDING ONION

Allium cernuum. A distinctive wild onion nods gracefully to forest visitors. It shows white or pink tepals, rounded at the tips. The stamens protrude beyond the tepals. Many individual flowers hang from slender pedicels, giving the inflorescence an exquisite starburst effect. The long, slender bulbs grow in clusters. It blooms in early summer. HABITAT: Moist but usually well-drained soils from low to high elevations. RANGE: Most mountainous regions of North America from Canada to Mexico, except for California and the Blue Mountains of E Oregon and Washington and adjacent Idaho.

DOUGLAS' ONION

Allium douglasii. Showy balls of deep pink to occasional white flowers crown round stems 4 to 16 inches high. Two or three papery bracts subtend each dense umbel, and many pink or yellowish stamens usually project beyond the acute tepals. Two leaves grow from each bulb. They may be narrow and grasslike or 1/2 inch or more wide, but shorter than the flower stem. The leaves remain green as the flowers bloom from May into July. HABITAT: Bunchgrass foothills and slopes into the lower mountains. RANGE: Generally peripheral to the Columbia Basin and barely into W Montana. COMMENT: Named for David Douglas, early explorer of the Pacific Northwest.

Lily Family *(Liliaceae)*

Lily Family *(Liliaceae)*

ROBINSON'S ONION

Allium robinsonii. This dwarf wild onion sends up a flattened flower stem only about 1 inch above ground. The white to pink or red tepals often give the umbel a variegated appearance above two purplish, papery bracts. Each flower in the tightly crowded umbel rests on a very short pedicel. Unlike many other species of *Allium*, the stamens remain enclosed within the blossom. Two flat, gracefully curving leaves grow considerably taller than the flowers. Early to mid spring is the time to look for this beautiful little sprite. HABITAT-RANGE: Endemic to the sandy or gravelly flats along the Columbia River from central Washington to the east end of the Columbia Gorge.

SIBERIAN CHIVES

Allium schoenoprasum. A tight umbellate head of lovely pink or rose-colored blooms surmount each of several smooth, round, hollow stems that grow in a clump, 8 to 18 inches high. Up to 30 individual flowers compose each floral cluster, cupped by two papery white bracts. Two grasslike leaves sheath the base of each flower stem and grow shorter than the stems. Look for this probable forerunner of cultivated garden chives from late spring to midsummer. HABITAT: Damp alpine and subalpine meadows and intermontane valleys. RANGE: Circumpolar in cold regions, south to N Oregon and Colorado. COMMENT: Wild onions are edible, but indiscriminate digging should be strictly discouraged. Without positive identification, one could mistakenly ingest death camas bulbs with dire results.

Lily Family *(Liliaceae)*

Lily Family *(Liliaceae)*

FORKTOOTH OOKOW, CLUSTER LILY

Brodiaea congesta. Six pale lavender or bluish tepals, nicely rounded at the ends, spread wide from a cup-shaped tube. Three sterile stamens, called staminodia, display forked ends and beautify the center of each flower. Several to many flowers cluster atop a 1 to 2 1/2 foot, slender, non-branching stem. Each flower attaches to the stem by a very short pedicel, creating an umbel. Two or three flattened, grasslike leaves stand nearly as tall as the flowers and remain green during blooming in late spring. HABITAT: Open, grassy or sometimes rocky areas at lower elevations. RANGE: Western Washington to central California and eastward in the Columbia Gorge.

DOUGLAS' BRODIAEA, WILD HYACINTH

Brodiaea douglasii. Six pale blue or medium blue tepals join at the base to form a floral tube about 1/2 inch long. The three outer tepals flare widely and three inner ones have ruffled edges that nearly close the mouth of the tube. Dark blue center stripes prettily mark the tepals. Six or more flowers sit atop tall, slender, leafless stems in an umbel. One or two linear, grassy leaves remain bright green at flowering time from April to June. HABITAT: Grassy prairies, sagebrush plains and open pine forests. RANGE: British Columbia, east of the Cascades, to W Montana and south to N Utah.

Lily Family *(Liliaceae)*

HOWELL'S BRODIAEA

Brodiaea howellii. Similar to Douglas' brodiaea, this species produces larger flowers, to 1 inch long, and generally very pale blue (almost white to sky blue). Each tepal has a dark blue midline. The outer three tepals (sepals) have smooth edges, while the inner ones (petals) display somewhat wavy (but not ruffled) margins. Smooth, unbranched stems grow about 2 feet tall, and two grass-like leaves normally reach about half the height of the blooms. The flowers appear from April to July. HABITAT: Quite good soil that dries out by summertime. RANGE: Eastern Cascades to the coast from S British Columbia to SW Oregon.

EARTH BRODIAEA

Brodiaea terrestris. Uncommon for a *Brodiaea*, this one grows quite low to the ground. The floral stem is only about 2 inches long and it originates well below ground. An umbel, usually of two to four flowers, tops the stem. Each flower perches on a very slender pedicel, 1 to 8 inches, which can be much longer than the stem. Six blue or purplish tepals surround a light-colored, triangular center. Three white, U-shaped, sterile stamens, called staminodia, form the corners of the triangle and tend to lean inward. They overtop and nearly enclose the three fertile stamens. The bloom lasts from late spring into summer. HABITAT: Sandy grassy areas to open woods along the immediate coast. RANGE: Southwestern Oregon to California.

Lily Family *(Liliaceae)*

HAIRY CAT'S EAR

Calochortus elegans. One to seven
flowers per plant display a greenish white
tinge outside and a purple cast on the
dense hairs within. Stylish purple
crescents decorate the inner faces of the
broad petals and the smaller sepals. Each
plant has just one long, fairly broad leaf
that overtops the flowers. This mariposa
(the name means "butterfly" in Spanish)
grows lowest and smallest of the dozen
or so species in the Northwest. Look for
it in late spring. HABITAT: Coniferous
forests and margins from medium to high
elevation. RANGE: Southeastern
Washington to W Montana to N
California.

Lily Family *(Liliaceae)*

Lily Family *(Liliaceae)*

GREEN BANDED STAR TULIP

Calochortus macrocarpus. This glorious
mariposa lily has three sharp, narrow sepals
that are generally longer than the petals.
The blooms range in color from white, as
shown, to, more commonly, lavender or
purple. A narrow, longitudinal green stripe
decorates the middle of each petal and
sepal, noticeable on the back if not on the
face. One to three flowers per plant appear
from late spring to summer, depending on
elevation. HABITAT: Dry open prairies to
moderately high elevations in the mountains.
RANGE: The Columbia Basin, S British
Columbia to NW Montana and south to N
Nevada and NE California.

Lily Family *(Liliaceae)*

LYALL'S STAR TULIP
Calochortus lyallii. Another small, hairy mariposa lily grows 4 to 12 inches tall. Three petals are broadly lance-shaped or oval and sharply pointed. A heavy fringe of hairs decorates the edges of the white or purplish petals. A dark purple crescent arches over a deep lunar gland at the base of each petal and the narrower sepals. From one to nine flowers form an umbel in the axils of a pair of upper bracts. One flat leaf, that grows about as high as the blooms, clasps the floral stem at the base. Look for this attractive flower in May and June. HABITAT: Open grassy hills to ponderosa pine forest. RANGE: East slope of the Cascades, S British Columbia to South-central Washington.

Lily Family *(Liliaceae)*

TOLMIE'S MARIPOSA LILY, PUSSY EARS

Calochortus tolmiei. The eye-catching appeal of this magnificent wildflower is the densely hairy petal faces that may vary from white to purple. The broad rounded petals reach from 1/2 to 1 1/2 inches in length—from medium size to the largest of our mariposa lilies. A raised gland arches near the base of each petal, but one must look beneath the hairy coating to see it. Normally one basal leaf reaches somewhat longer than the floral stem and is up to 1 inch wide. The stem may also bear one or more smaller leaves. In fruit the stems turn downward. April to July for this one. HABITAT: Rocky or sandy soil of meadows or brushy hills. RANGE: Willamette Valley to the coast and south to central California.

Lily Family *(Liliaceae)*

Lily Family *(Liliaceae)*

LEICHTLIN'S CAMAS
Camassia leichtlinii. Leichtlin's camas grows 2 feet tall or more and produces numerous leaves 1 inch wide. The deep set bulbs are about 1 inch in diameter and quite edible. Flower color varies from creamy white to deep blue. The six tepals are arranged in a symmetrical, open face, 2 to 3 inches in diameter. As the tepals wither, they twist tightly together until forced open by the expanding fruit capsule. These beautiful flowers bloom in spring. HABITAT: Deep moist soil of meadows and slopes. RANGE: Vancouver Island to SW Oregon, west of the Cascades and in the California Sierras. COMMENT: Botanists recognize two varieties; a white one, *leichtlinii*, in SW Oregon, shown here, and a blue variety, *suksdorfii*, in the rest of the range.

CAMAS, BLUE CAMASS, WILD HYACINTH
Camassia quamash. Camas flowers may vary from pale blue to deep purple or occasionally white (albino). Numerous blossoms attach on short peduncles (a raceme) to smooth, slender, upright stems, 8 to 24 inches tall. They open a few at a time from the bottom upward, revealing six narrow, spreading tepals and six prominent blue or yellow stamens. Three or four grasslike leaves sheath the base of the plant. Six varieties of this camas glorify the Northwest in springtime. HABITAT: Loves moist meadows, but also grassy sagebrush flats and even fairly heavily timbered hillsides with deep soil. RANGE: British Columbia and Alberta to California and Wyoming. COMMENTS: Camas bulbs were a vegetable staple of Indians in the Pacific Northwest before the arrival of white people. Some camas meadows in Idaho appeared to William Clark, of Lewis and Clark fame, to "resemble a lake of fine clear water, so complete in this deception that on first sight I could have sworn it was water."

QUEEN'S CUP, BEAD LILY

Clintonia uniflora. This stylish white lily spreads six pearly tepals, about 1 inch across, in the shape of an open bell. The solitary flower terminates a peduncle about 4 inches high, naked except for a small linear bract near the top. Two or three glossy green, broadly oval and parallel-veined leaves compose a perfect setting for the blossom on the forest floor. Queen's cup blooms in early summer and a round, blue berry develops in late summer. HABITAT: Deep forests at low to mid elevations. RANGE: Alaska to Montana and California. COMMENT: One generally finds more white flowers than other colors in deep woods because white is best for attracting bees and other pollinating insects in forest shade.

Lily Family *(Liliaceae)*

Lily Family *(Liliaceae)*

HOOKER'S FAIRYBELL, OREGON FAIRYBELL

Disporum hookeri. Two or three creamy flowers, narrowly bell-shaped and spreading at the open end, hang from stem ends on short petioles. They arise from the axils of a pair of terminal leaves that tend to hide the blossoms. The broad, lance-shaped or heart-shaped leaves clasp the stems at their bases. The plants grow 1 to 2 feet tall and the stems branch sparingly. Red or orangish berries develop in late summer. Blooming occurs in spring and early summer. HABITAT: Deep, wet woods and stream banks. RANGE: British Columbia and Alberta to W Montana and N Oregon in the Cascades. COMMENT: Wartberry fairybell, *D. trachycarpum*, looks much like this one and resides in the Rockies.

36

Lily Family *(Liliaceae)*

SMITH'S FAIRYBELL, FAIRY LANTERNS

Disporum smithii. This lush herb sends up stems 1 to 3 feet long that branch numerous times. Broad shiny leaves, 2 to 5 inches long, clasp the stems at their bases and narrow abruptly to sharp points at the tip. One to several cylindrical flowers attach at the ends of the stems and usually hang beneath the terminal leaves. The creamy tepals do not flare appreciably and completely enclose the stamens and stigmas. It blooms in spring. Smooth, yellowish to orange-red berries develop in summer. HABITAT: A denizen of moist, shady woods. RANGE: Coast Range and western slope of the Cascades, British Columbia to California.

Lily Family *(Liliaceae)*

GLACIER LILY, DOGTOOTH VIOLET

Erythronium grandiflorum. One or more nodding blossoms spread six brilliant yellow tepals that often curve gracefully backward from a smooth green stem 6 to 12 inches high. Two broad, oval leaves grow from the base. Six conspicuous anthers may vary from white to yellow, red or purple. Glacier lilies sometimes grow in masses in alpine meadows, creating breathtaking natural gardens. The blooms emerge soon after snow melt from March to August. HABITAT: Varies widely from low valleys to moderately dense forests to alpine heights. RANGE: Southern British Columbia and Alberta, south to Oregon and Colorado.

Lily Family *(Liliaceae)*

Lily Family *(Liliaceae)*

AVALANCHE LILY, ALPINE FAWN LILY

Erythronium montanum. Two glossy green leaves, narrowly oval and pointed on the ends, arise at the base of this plant, the lower leaf clasping the base of the upper. Growing in masses on optimum sites, avalanche lily can turn mountain sides snowy white. The creamy tepals curl gracefully backward from yellow bases. Yellow anthers add their accents to the glorious blooms. The flowers appear from May into August, depending on snow melt. HABITAT: Subalpine forest to alpine meadows. RANGE: Vancouver Island to the Olympics and Cascades of Washington and Mt. Hood in Oregon. COMMENT: *Erythronium* has many common names such as dogtooth violet, trout lily, fawn lily and adder's tongue. All parts of the plants are edible, and bears frequently feed on them early in spring.

COAST FAWN LILY, TROUT LILY

Erythronium revolutum. Another spectacular *Erythronium* may vary in color from dark pink to magenta or purple with a yellow or dark center. The plants usually possess just one nodding blossom, but occasionally may put forth two to five. As the name *revolutum* implies, the tepals reflex or curl backward. Two leaves, 3 to 5 inches long, show beautiful purplish mottling, which gives rise to the common name, fawn lily. It blooms in spring. HABITAT: Coastal forest to fringes and openings from low elevations to mountain tops. RANGE: Southern British Columbia to NW California in the Coast Range. COMMENT: Coast fawn lily appears on rare or sensitive species lists and should not be picked or transplanted.

Lily Family *(Liliaceae)*

OREGON TROUT LILY

Erythronium oregonum. Large, lustrous white or pinkish flowers, with tepals about 1 1/2 inches long, show pretty yellow accents in the centers. From one to three blossoms may grow on a naked stem to 12 inches high. The leaves merit as much attention as the flowers. They are glossy smooth, oblong or lance-shaped, to 8 inches long and brilliantly mottled with brown or purple areas that form distinctive patterns. They bloom in spring. HABITAT: Open prairies to moist but well-drained forests, preferring lower elevations. RANGE: British Columbia through Puget Sound and Willamette Valley to SW Oregon.

Lily Family *(Liliaceae)*

SISKIYOU FRITILLARY

Fritillaria glauca. A single, bowl-shaped flower, strikingly camouflaged in greenish yellow and purple mottling, nods a greeting to its visitors. The surprisingly large blossom perches on a low stem only 4 or 5 inches high. One must sink to one's knees to fully savor the unique coloring and the six yellow stamens surrounding a three-part stigma. Three alternate leaves usually sprout from the stem. They are lance- or oval-shaped, quite deeply channeled and bear a bluish, glaucous coating. Look for these enchanting blooms in spring. HABITAT: Rocky or gravelly serpentine slopes or stream banks. RANGE: Endemic to the Siskiyou Mountains of SW Oregon and NW California. COMMENT: Siskiyou fritillary is classed as rare and endangered in Oregon, but is more abundant in California. Three other *Fritillaria*, one a scarlet species, inhabit SW Oregon and rate rare and endangered classifications.

Lily Family *(Liliaceae)*

Lily Family *(Liliaceae)*

MISSION BELLS, CHECKER LILY

Fritillaria lanceolata. One or more spectacular, broadly cup-shaped blossoms hang pendent on an unbranching stem, 4 to 40 inches tall. The flowers are gloriously mottled in various shades of purple, yellow and green and open about 1 1/2 inches across. Smooth, narrow leaves may form one or two whorls near mid stem or alternate upward. Early April to June for this one. HABITAT: Open grassy spaces to wooded areas from low elevation to moderate heights in the mountains. RANGE: Southern British Columbia to N Idaho, the Washington Cascades and the Coast Range from Oregon to S California.

YELLOW BELL

Fritillaria pudica. These pretty yellow harbingers of spring rise 4 to 10 inches tall from a small scaly bulb. One to three pendent, bell-shaped flowers identify this perennial. The flowers may turn orange to dull red with age. Two or more linear or oblong and smooth leaves originate on the floral stem. It blooms early, March to June depending on elevation. HABITAT: Grassy meadows and prairies, sagebrush deserts where moist in the spring, to open forests and subalpine ridges. RANGE: British Columbia, east of the Cascades, and Alberta, south to W Colorado and NE California.

Lily Family *(Liliaceae)*

Lily Family *(Liliaceae)*

SAND LILY, STAR LILY

Leucocrinum montanum. Several startling white lilies nestle in a clump of linear, grasslike leaves, 8 inches long or less. The leaves are somewhat white-margined and channeled in cross section. Both the leaves and flowers originate well below ground from a thick root crown. Six narrowly lance-shaped tepals cohere at the base and form a floral tube 2 to 3 inches long. Six yellow stamens supply a color accent in the floral center. The seeds of sand lily form below ground level. Blooms erupt in spring. HABITAT: Well-drained soil from sagebrush prairies to fairly dense forest in the mountains. RANGE: Central Oregon and N California to the Dakotas and New Mexico. COMMENT: *Leucocrinum* has just this one species.

WASHINGTON LILY, CASCADE LILY

Lilium washintonianum. Upright stems 2 to 5 feet tall exalt these impressive, 3 to 5 inch long, trumpet-shaped lilies. From a long floral tube, six tepals spread wide or reflex moderately. White or pinkish at first and often dippled with purple spots, they fade to pink or purple with age. The leaves form whorls along the middle of the stem, but are single and alternate below and sometimes above. The blossoms appear from early to mid-summer. HABITAT: Brush fields and forest openings to moderate elevations. RANGE: The Oregon Cascades through the California Sierras. COMMENT: At least a half-dozen species of spectacular lilies inhabit the SW corner of Oregon into California. Most of them are considered rare or endangered.

Lily Family *(Liliaceae)*

COLUMBIA LILY, TIGER LILY

Lilium columbianum. A stunning, classical lily unfolds six orange tepals, gloriously spotted with red or purple and strongly recurved backward. The plants lift two to twenty of these blossoms 2 to 4 feet high. The smooth, elliptical leaves appear whorled or scattered on the stalk. Look for this gorgeous wildflower in late spring or early summer. HABITAT: Coniferous woods and forest margins to open areas, low to moderately high elevation. RANGE: British Columbia to California in the Cascades and east to NW Montana and Nevada. COMMENT: "Consider the lilies of the field, how they grow, they neither toil nor spin; yet I tell you, even Solomon in all his glory was not arrayed like one of these." (Matthew 6:28)

Lily Family *(Liliaceae)*

Lily Family *(Liliaceae)*

FALSE LILY OF THE VALLEY

Maianthemum dilatatum. Upright racemes of tiny white flowers each possess four petals, making an exception to the rule of threes and sixes in the lily family. Two or three distinctive leaves grow on the floral stems. They are about as wide as long, heart- or arrow-shaped and supported by rather long, slender petioles. The plants spread by underground rhizomes and create solid masses of ground cover on favorable sites. Look for the blooms in spring. HABITAT: Moist soil in wooded areas. RANGE: Alaska to California, Coast and Cascade Ranges and across British Columbia to N Idaho.

FALSE SOLOMON SEAL

Smilacina racemosa. A multitude of tiny white flowers covers the branches of a panicle. The individual blossoms disappear in the mass of the inflorescence without very close inspection. They are nearly sessile or rest on very short pedicels. The main stem reaches 12 to 40 inches long and rises from a strong, shallow rhizome. Broadly lance-shaped leaves, 3 to 8 inches long and sharp-pointed on the end, attach merely sessile or clasp the stem. They are noticeably parallel-veined. Red berries develop in the fall. It blooms in spring and early summer. HABITAT: A denizen of forests and open woods on moist soil. RANGE: Most of Canada and continental United States.

STAR FLOWERED SOLOMON PLUME

Smilacina stellata. Star flowered Solomon plume or Solomon seal is a smaller plant than the previous one. The stems grow 8 to 24 inches and they sometimes zigzag from leaf node to leaf node. The leaves are generally narrower and shorter than false Solomon seal. Although the flowers are relatively few in number, one quite readily notices the individual blooms with six narrow tepals. This one also spreads by underground rhizomes. The flowers open in May and June. HABITAT: Moist forests to open, often rocky slopes. RANGE: Most of forested North America.

Lily Family *(Liliaceae)*

Lily Family *(Liliaceae)*

TWISTED STALK

Streptopus amplexifolius. Broad, lance-shaped leaves, 3 or 4 inches long, clasp the stems of this smooth, leafy plant, 1 1/2 to 3 feet tall. Several branches originate in leaf axils. Small bell-shaped, cream-colored flowers hang pendent along the stem on rather long pedicels, which have distinct kinks at midlength. The fruit are smooth, oval berries, normally red but sometimes yellow. One may easily overlook the flowers or berries concealed beneath the leaves. Blooms open in May and June. HABITAT: Look for twisted stalk on wet stream banks in woods and thickets. RANGE: Most of North America, north of Mexico.

45

Lily Family *(Liliaceae)*

BRONZE BELLS

Stenanthium occidentale. From a small bulb this plant raises several grasslike leaves and a slender stem that may or may not branch in the inflorescence. The flowers resemble small bells with six flaring, sharp-pointed tepals and tend to decorate just one side of the stem. They normally hang pendent from pedicels up to 1 inch long and vary in color from greenish yellow to bronze or brownish red. The blossoms appear from mid to late summer. HABITAT: Rocky slopes, meadows or stream banks, mostly subalpine or alpine, but sea level upward on the Olympic Peninsula and Columbia Gorge. RANGE: British Columbia and Alberta to N California, Montana and Idaho. COMMENT: We have just one species in W North America.

Lily Family *(Liliaceae)*

Lily Family *(Liliaceae)*

FALSE ASPHODEL, STICKY TOFIELDIA

Tofieldia glutinosa. Sticky, gland-tipped hairs *(glutinosa)* coat the straight un-branched stems that reach 4 to 20 inches high. Headlike clusters of tiny white or greenish flowers show minute spots of purple or brown supplied by the stamens. The grassy leaves sheath stem bases and may ascend part way up the stems, depending upon the variety. Search for these miniature lilies in summer. HABITAT: Prefers wet or marshy places with limestone or calcareous substrate from low to alpine elevations; mostly high altitude in our region. RANGE: Alaska, across Canada and south to California and Colorado in the west. COMMENT: One can find five varieties of false asphodel.

WESTERN TRILLIUM, WAKE ROBIN

Trillium ovatum. Western trillium displays three exquisite petals about 2 inches long, pearly white at the peak of bloom, but often turning pink or dull red with age. Three green sepals, nearly as long as the petals but much narrower, alternate with the petals. Six yellow anthers highlight the floral center. The solitary flower surmounts a whorl of three or more sessile leaves that duplicate the general shape of the petals but are larger and nearly as broad as long. Trillium blooms early, soon after snow melt. HABITAT: Conifer forests where moist or boggy in the spring. RANGE: British Columbia to SW Alberta, south to Colorado and N California. COMMENT: We have three species of trillium in the Northwest.

47

Lily Family *(Liliaceae)*

PURPLE TRILLIUM

Trillium petiolatum. Nestling at ground line in the juncture of three long-petioled leaves, a purple trillium flower can easily go unnoticed. The stem grows underground, 2 to 5 inches long. Round or broadly oval leaf blades stretch 3 to 5 inches across, the leaf petioles originating from the stem beneath the flowers. The blossom has no separate floral stem. Three greenish, oblong sepals reach 1 to 2 1/2 inches in length, while the yellowish green to purple or brown petals grow somewhat larger. They often twist or curl. Blooming occurs in spring. HABITAT: Moist forests, streambanks and meadows. RANGE: East slope of the Cascades in central Washington to the Blue Mountains in NE Oregon and the NW edge of Idaho. COMMENT: Giant trillium, *T. chloropetalum,* bears similarly shaped flowers but on a plant resembling western trillium in W Oregon and Washington.

Lily Family *(Liliaceae)*

Lily Family *(Liliaceae)*

FALSE HELLEBORE

Veratrum californicum. Stout stalks, which do not branch below the inflorescence, stand 4 to 6 feet tall, and numerous parallel-veined leaves, 8 to 10 inches long, clasp the stems. The flowers create an elongated mass of small, off-white blossoms on lateral, spreading branches as well as the tip of the main stem. False hellebore blooms in summer. HABITAT: Wet places in woods and meadows from low to high altitude. RANGE: Western Washington to W Montana and south to New Mexico and Mexico.

INDIAN HELLEBORE, GREEN CORN LILY

Veratrum viride. Indian hellebore has the same general proportions as false hellebore, the stems reaching 3 to 6 feet. Leaves at the base, oblong and strongly parallel-veined, clasp the stem, and grow 10 to 14 inches long. Upper stem leaves reduce in size. Branches of the inflorescence droop markedly, especially the lower ones. Individual flowers reach 1/4 to 1/2 inch across. Six stamens rest in the center of six rounded tepals, all green or greenish yellow in color. They bloom in summer and early fall. HABITAT: Moist or boggy ground from open meadows to dense thickets, mostly in the mountains. RANGE: Alaska to E Canada and south to N Oregon Cascades, Montana and North Carolina. COMMENT: Both species are quite poisonous to livestock.

Lily Family *(Liliaceae)*

BEARGRASS

Xerophyllum tenax. These flowers rise like tall stately sentinels, 2 to 3 feet or more. A multitude of slender pedicels about 2 inches long individually support a large round mass or conical plume of small, creamy white flowers. Each blossom spreads six snowy tepals and projects six stamens. The plants do not bloom every year—perhaps once in seven years or so under a forest canopy, but more frequently on open sites. In a good year beargrass can be breathtaking. Spreading by thick woody rhizomes, the plants develop dense tussocks of coarse, grasslike leaves that have rough edges and are slippery under foot. They may cover open hillsides or grow sparsely in forested areas. Blooms from June to early August. HABITAT: Fairly dense forest at medium elevation to open alpine slopes. RANGE: British Columbia and Alberta to Wyoming and California. COMMENT: Beargrass is the official flower of Glacier National Park. Rocky mountain goats eat the tough evergreen leaves in winter and many game animals feed on the succulent flower buds and stems in spring. In the early days Indians wove baskets, clothing and utensils from the coarse leaves.

Lily Family *(Liliaceae)*

Lily Family *(Liliaceae)*

MOUNTAIN DEATH CAMAS

Zigadenus elegans. Six tepals open wide, creating a star-shaped blossom about 3/4 inch across. A heart-shaped gland at the base of each petal makes a greenish yellow, scalloped decoration around the center of each creamy white flower. The stems may or may not branch in the inflorescence. Several bright green linear leaves, 4 to 10 inches long, and a single floral stem, usually 1 to 2 feet tall, erupt from a single bulb. Blooming occurs from early in the season to midsummer. HABITAT: Most common in alpine meadows, but may also inhabit valleys at medium elevation. RANGE: Alaska to W Washington and through the Rockies to N Mexico. COMMENT: All species of *Zigadenus* should be considered deadly poisonous to animals and humans alike.

PANICLED DEATH CAMAS

Zigadenus paniculata. The flowers of panicled death camas closely resemble those of meadow death camas, *Z. venenosus,* except that they form a panicle (they branch in the inflorescence) instead of a raceme. Other technical features also differentiate the two species. The stem may reach 20 inches high and the shorter, mostly basal leaves 1/2 inch wide. They bloom in spring. HABITAT: Open grassy or sagebrush prairies and slopes to piney woods. RANGE: East slope of the Cascades in central Washington to central Montana, New Mexico and the California Sierras.

Orchid Family *(Orchidaceae)*

FAIRYSLIPPER

Calypso bulbosa. Among the world's flowers, the orchids must surely rank among the most enchanting. Not all of our orchids have spectacular blossoms, but fairyslipper does. The overall color varies from white or cream to, more commonly, pale pink to deep magenta. One inflated petal forms the slipper, tipped with two horn-like projections under the toe. Exquisite purple stripes decorate the slipper inside and below and bright yellow hairs and purple spots adorn the top. Two other petals and three sepals, all narrow and sharp-pointed, effect a starry purple crown. Above the slipper opening hangs a rounded hood, which is the "column," a feature common to all orchids. Fused stamens and styles com-

prise the column, arranged so that only insects can pollinate the flowers. Each plant sends up a single stem, 2 to 8 inches high, clasped by two or three bracts. One broad, oval leaf emerges in the fall from a rounded corm and over-winters under the snow. Fairyslipper blooms early in the season, soon after snow melt. HABITAT: Moist woods with a layer of duff, from the sea coast to moderate elevations in the mountains. RANGE: Transcontinental, Alaska and Canada and south to NE United States, New Mexico and California. COMMENT: Calypso can be locally abundant, but logging has destroyed vast areas of its habitat. All orchids should be considered rare or endangered and should never be picked or transplanted.

Orchid Family *(Orchidaceae)*

Orchid Family *(Orchidaceae)*

SPOTTED CORALROOT

Corallorhiza maculata. The coralroots possess no green leaves and are variously classed as saprophytes or parasites. Saprophytes rely on decayed organic material for sustenance. Technically, coralroots are parasites on specific fungi that decay organic matter in the forest floor. These fascinating orchids send up numerous stems, 8 to 18 inches tall, from spreading underground rhizomes. Several bracts clasp the yellow to purple or brownish stems. An open, spike-like raceme of 10 to 30 flowers occupies the upper 1/2 to 1/3 of the stem. A yellow, tubular ovary forms the basal half of the flower. Three reddish to purple sepals and two upper petals arch gracefully over and around the lower lip formed by the third petal. Wine red or purple spots embellish the lip, which is white or pale pink. The two upper petals may also be spotted, but less noticeably. Albino specimens occur frequently and may easily be mistaken for yellow coralroot, *C. trifida.* Blooms from May to August. HABITAT: Woods and forests. RANGE: Transcontinental in the United States and S Canada.

MERTEN'S CORALROOT

Corallorhiza mertensiana. Captivating beauty glorifies the pendulous lip petals of this little coralroot. Pink to deep red, unspotted, but sometimes with a white tip, two teeth on the sides and darker stripes, the lip petal identifies this one unmistakably. Two narrow sepals, brownish or red, spread wide on the sides. Above, two petals and one sepal fuse together for most of their length and make a narrow hood. Inside the hood an upright, slender, light-colored column of fused stamens and styles arches gracefully outward and forms an entrance to the spur. Several slender stems commonly grow in a clump and stand 6 to 18 inches tall. Look for them to bloom in summer. HABITAT: Moist coniferous forest. RANGE: Alaska to Montana and south to California and Wyoming.

Orchid Family *(Orchidaceae)*

Orchid Family *(Orchidaceae)*

STRIPED CORALROOT

Corallorhiza striata. Striped coralroot stands 6 to 16 inches tall, has several clasping bracts on purplish stems and a spikelike raceme of up to 30 flowers on the upper half of the stem. A lower petal which forms an enlarged lip, is deep maroon to purple and concave with thickened margins. Two other petals and three sepals, usually pinkish with three red to purple stripes, droop gracefully over the lip. This one blooms from mid-spring to early summer. HABITAT: Deep moist woods. RANGE: Across Canada and south in the western mountains to Mexico. COMMENT: Never very abundant.

PHANTOM ORCHID

Eburophyton austinae. A strange, spellbinding ghost on the forest floor, phantom orchid is sheer white or ivory-color overall, turning brown with age. It lacks green leaves and is therefore a saprophyte, relying on a fungus in its roots to obtain sustenance from decaying organic matter in the soil. The plants stand 8 to 20 inches tall, the leaves reduced to mere silvery, clasping bracts. The lower petal forms a small open sac and has a yellowish spot in the throat, the only color on the plant. The petals and sepals, about 3/4 inch long and narrowly elliptical, shield or cup the short lip and column. Blooms from June to early August. HABITAT: Well-drained, medium-dense forest. RANGE: Idaho to the Pacific Coast, Washington to California. COMMENT: *Eburophyton* has only one known species.

Orchid Family *(Orchidaceae)*

YELLOW LADYSLIPPER

Cypripedium calceolus. These gaudy orchids possess one petal unmistakably shaped like a slipper, about 1 inch long. As a group, the ladyslippers display one centered sepal, two smaller petals above the slipper and two fused sepals underneath. In this species the three upper tepals twist enchantingly and show shades of yellowish-greenish-purple with darker purple, parallel stripes. The bright yellow triangular column, spotted with red or purple, arches downward, leading insects into the slipper opening. Yellow ladyslipper normally supports just one blossom that crowns a leafy stem 6 to 16 inches high. The elliptic leaves reach 2 1/2 to 7 inches long and arise mostly on the lower stem. The flower rests on a short peduncle that springs form the axil of a small upper bract that usually overtops the flower. The blooms open in May and June. HABITAT: Mossy stream banks and wet woods. RANGE: Widespread in boreal forests of the N hemisphere. Rare in the Northwest east of the Cascades and apparently extinct now in Oregon.

Orchid Family *(Orchidaceae)*

CLUSTERED LADYSLIPPER

Cyripedium fasciculatum. A cluster of two to four small flowers crowns this rare ladyslipper. Each blossom has a 1/2 inch long pouch, mottled greenish and purplish. Three tepals, 1/2 to 1 inch long, reddish purple and pointed at the tip, hover over the slipper, while two lower tepals join together and appear as one. Long woolly hairs clothe the stems, 2 to 8 inches high, and a pair of oval, green or purplish leaves subtend the flowers at or well above mid height. The flowers open from May into summer. HABITAT: Dense, moist forest to drier open stands. RANGE: South-central British Columbia to N Idaho, Colorado, and N California.

Orchid Family *(Orchidaceae)*　　　　Orchid Family *(Orchidaceae)*

MOUNTAIN LADYSLIPPER

Cypripedium montanum. The queen of
the ladyslippers! The lower petal inflates
broadly into a lustrous white pouch or
slipper, about 1 inch long, prominently
ribbed, sometimes with purplish veins.
The tepals very closely resemble those
of yellow ladyslipper. A brilliant yellow
column, usually spotted red or purple,
accents the throat of the slipper. These
plants stand 1 to 2 feet tall, have one to
three blossoms and numerous broadly
oval, luxuriant, parallel-veined leaves.
The blossoms emerge from the axils of
the upper leaves that clasp the stem.
Look for these breathtaking beauties
mostly in June. It will make your day to
find them. HABITAT: Moist but well-
drained mountain slopes and woods.
RANGE: Alaska to Alberta, Wyoming
and N California.

WHITE BOG ORCHID

Habenaria dilatata. Stately unbranched
stems stand 1/2 to 3 feet tall. Luxurious,
lance-shaped leaves clasp the stem at the
base and grow smaller and sessile upward.
A dense spike of white, fragrant orchids,
about 1/2 inch across, clothe the upper
stem. The pure white lip droops gracefully
in front and curves backward and downward into a slender hollow spur. One sepal
and two petals create a hood over the lip,
and two sepals spread wide on the sides.
Blooms in summer. HABITAT: Wet ground
or bogs. RANGE: Northern North America,
south to New Mexico and California.
COMMENT: All orchids must be pollinated
by insects. They never self-pollinate. Many
species have evolved special shapes and
structures to coincide with the size, shape
and habits of specific insects. The life
cycles of orchids and insects are often
interdependent. Orchid pollination presents
a fascinating field of study.

In *Habenaria* the spur holds nectar on
which insects feed. Only insects with long,
flexible tongues, usually moths, can reach
the nectar. Directly above the opening to
the spur sits the column coated with
pollen. An insect's forehead comes in
contact with the pollen when it sticks its
tongue into the spur.

Orchid Family *(Orchidaceae)*

GIANT HELLEBORINE, CHATTERBOX

Epipactis gigantea. Should one chance upon this exquisite orchid, take time to observe it closely and relish the superb design. Three greenish sepals, burnished with copper tones and veined with darker lines, frame three more colorful petals. Two upper petals, smaller than the sepals, blush with a pretty pink outside and repeat the purple veins of the sepals inside. The third petal forms an open sac or lip, gorgeously striped with red or purple inside. Three lobes embellish the outer lip—a terminal pinkish or yellowish tongue has inrolled margins and supports two triangular, upright teeth, striped with red or brown, that partially closes the sac. When one touches the plant, these teeth vibrate, leading to the common name, chatterbox.

Several lance-shaped leaves sheathe the stem, which usually stands 1 to 2 1/2 feet tall but may reach 5 feet on ideal growing sites. The plants spread by underground rhizomes and may form extensive colonies. Blooming occurs from April to July. HABITAT: Wet or marshy ground from desert regions to wooded areas. RANGE: Southern British Columbia to the Black Hills and south to W Texas and much of Mexico. COMMENT: Giant helleborine occurs infrequently and is considered rare over much of its range.

Orchid Family *(Orchidaceae)*   **Orchid Family** *(Orchidaceae)*

SLENDER (GREEN) BOG ORCHID

Habenaria saccata. On this orchid the lip petal projects backward and down, forming a round or somewhat tubular sac under the lip. The sac grows only about 2/3 the length of the lip and therefore tends to hide from view. The unbranching stems reach 12 to 30 inches or more and have two sheathing bracts at the base. Lower stem leaves assume oblong or oval shapes, quite rounded on the ends, becoming narrower and more pointed upward. In the lower inflorescence the leaves reduce to mere bracts, almost grasslike. Look for these yellowish green flower spikes in early to midsummer. HABITAT: Wet or marshy places from low to subalpine elevations. RANGE: Alaska to Alberta, N California and New Mexico. COMMENT: We have about a half-dozen species of green bog orchids, at least two of which prefer dry growing sites instead of bogs.

FROG ORCHIS

Habenaria viridis. The common name, frog orchis, comes from the resemblance of the flower to a frog's face. The sepals and upper petals create a hood over the tiny column, while the lip petal droops and looks like a frog's tongue. The lip extends about 1/3 inch and has either two or three lobes at the tip. An inconspicuous spur forms a sac behind the frog's face. The overall green color may show a purplish tinge. Simple, smooth leaves sheathe the stem near the base and leafy bracts subtend the nearly sessile flowers. June and July for this one. HABITAT: Forests and open mountain slopes to subalpine. RANGE: Boreal forests of the N hemisphere, south in North America to Washington, New Mexico, Illinois and North Carolina.

Orchid Family *(Orchidaceae)*

ROUND LEAVED ORCHIS

Orchis rotundifolia. Several small flowers erupt from the axils of little green or purplish bracts in a crowded raceme. Each exquisite blossom sports three white or pinkish sepals. An upper sepal forms a rounded hood, while two winglike sepals spread wide on the sides. Two narrow, pink petals blend with the hood. The lower lip petal attracts immediate attention. It reaches about 1/3 inch in length and displays a small lobe on each side before spreading to a broad tongue. Red or purplish spots or streaks emblazon the lip petal. Spreading by rhizomes below or stolons above ground, the stems rise 4 to 8 inches. A couple of papery bracts sheathe the stem base below one sheathing basal leaf, which is broadly oval to nearly round and about 3 or 4 inches long. It blooms in early summer. HABITAT: Damp or wet woods, often on calcareous substrate. RANGE: Across subartic North America, south to S British Columbia, Montana and the Great Lakes. COMMENT: We have just this one species of *Orchis.* It is rare wherever it occurs and should never be picked or transplanted.

Cattail Family *(Typhaceae)*

Sedge Family *(Cyperaceae)*

COMMON CATTAIL

Typha latifolia. One of our most common, well-known and easily recognized wild plants, cattails propagate readily by thick, edible rhizomes. Dense stands of smooth, narrow leaves reach 3 to 9 feet high. Flowering stalks reach approximately the same height as the leaves. Tiny flowers form a dense column about 1 inch in diameter and 1 foot tall at the tip of the stalk. Staminate or male flowers make a fuzzy, light-colored appearance at the top half of the column and pistillate or female flowers occupy the lower half. After the pollen has fallen, the staminate flowers blow away on the wind, leaving only the dark brown column of pistillate flowers. Eventually they, too, develop fuzzy tails and disperse on the wind. Blooming occurs through summer into fall. HABITAT: Wet ground or shallow water with a muddy bottom. RANGE: Most of the N hemisphere south of the arctic and N Africa. COMMENT: A second species, *T. angustifolia*, normally grows smaller and an inch or two of bare stem separates the staminate and pistillate flowers.

COTTON GRASS

Eriophorum polystachion. Most members of the huge sedge family resemble grasses. The cotton sedges in bloom, however, are unmistakable. Each flowering stem may sport from two to eight spikelets, composed of many white, cottony bristles. Several brownish scales subtend each spikelet and the spikelets erupt from the axil formed by two or more leafy bracts, unequal in length. Several grasslike leaves sheath the 8 to 24 inch (or more) stem. The plants spread by rhizomes and create close colonies in favorable locations. July and August. HABITAT: Cold marshy ground, middle to alpine elevations. RANGE: Circumpolar in arctic regions and south to Oregon, N New Mexico, Michigan and Maine.

Sumac Family *(Anacardiaceae)*

Parsley Family *(Apiaceae, Umbelliferae)*

POISON OAK, POISON IVY

Rhus diversiloba. Anyone who has suffered a burning skin rash from the slightly volatile oil of poison oak or poison ivy will shy away from any future contact with them. Poison oak varies considerably from low shrubs to climbing vines, 40 feet long or more. The old adage "leaflets three, let it be" holds true for anyone unsure of a plant's identity. The poison oak shown here has three shiny green leaflets, entire and well rounded. However, they can also be lobed *(diversiloba)* and abruptly sharp-pointed. The flowers are very tiny and form open, branching panicles. Blooms appear April to July. HABITAT: Commonly in woods and thickets. RANGE: West slope of the Cascades to the coast, Washington to Mexico and through the Columbia Gorge. COMMENT: Poison ivy, *R. radicans,* dwells from E Oregon and Washington to the East Coast and south to Mexico. It has rather long, pointed leaflets and grows as a low shrub in our area, but more often as a climbing vine farther east. Two other members of the sumac family in the Northwest do not emit toxic oil.

LYALL'S ANGELICA

Angelica arguta. Coarse plants 3 to 7 feet tall exhibit many tiny white flowers in one or more flat-topped compound umbels (twice umbellate). The plants usually have two or three doubly pinnate leaves. Leaf bases clasp the unbranched main stem and the leaf petioles develop broad leafy wings up to the first pinnate node. Sharp irregular teeth line the edges of the leaflets. The flowers open in midsummer. HABITAT: Moist places in the valleys and mountains. RANGE: Southern British Columbia and Alberta to Utah and N California. COMMENT: Lyall's angelica is not reported to be poisonous, but several other members of the parsley family can be deadly for humans and livestock.

Parsley Family *(Apiaceae)*

DAWSON'S ANGELICA

Angelica dawsonii. Dawson's is quite distinctive and perhaps the most colorful of the *Angelicas*. Normally a single dense, compound umbel of pale or bright yellow flowers sits atop a whorl of sharply toothed bracts. The stem ascends 1 to 4 feet from a strong taproot. Large, pinnately compound basal leaves rest on long petioles, the leaflets lance-shaped and sharply serrated. Upper stem leaves grow considerably smaller. Early summer blooming for this one. HABITAT: Moist meadows and slopes, upper montane to subalpine. RANGE: The S Canadian Rockies to N Idaho and NW Montana.

WATER HEMLOCK

Cicuta douglasii. This native plant is deadly poisonous to livestock and humans. One can positively identify it by the veins of the leaflets which end at the bottom of the clefts between the teeth instead of at the tip of each tooth. The leaves are pinnately compound, the leaflets may also be two-lobed. The hollow, swollen base of the stem also has cross-walls that make several chambers—another positive identifier. A single stem or several stems from a single root may grow 2 to 6 feet tall. Summertime for this one. HABITAT: Wet places in woods and open stream banks. RANGE: Western North America, Alaska to Mexico. COMMENT: Poison hemlock, *Conium maculatum*, an alien from Europe, has more finely divided leaves and the hollow, branching stems are mottled with purple splotches. It, too, is extremely poisonous.

Parsley Family *(Apiaceae)*

63

Parsley Family *(Apiaceae)*

Parsley Family *(Apiaceae)*

BEACH SILVERTOP

Glehnia leiocarpa. From a strong perennial taproot a rosette of basal leaves sheaths a short floral stem beneath the surface of sand. The rather thick, leathery leaves, smooth above and hairy below, lie mostly prostrate on the sand. The pinnately compound leaves have broad, irregularly 3-lobed leaflets with small, mostly rounded teeth. Both floral stems and leaf petioles wear a dense coat of straight hairs. The compound umbel (twice umbellate) produces 5 to 13 primary rays and tight, headlike secondary umbels. The tiny greenish-white flowers become dry seeds in fruit, surrounded by numerous corky ridges, tinted purple in the photograph. They bloom from May to July. HABITAT: Coastal sand dunes and sandy flats. RANGE: Alaska to N California.

COW PARSNIP

Heracleum lanatum. Coarse plants, 3 to 9 feet high, spread 3-bladed, pinnate leaves to 1 foot across. The basal leaves are much larger than the upper ones, the leaflets palmately lobed (maple-like) and sharply toothed on the margins. Leafy wings flank the primary leaf petioles. Large, flat-topped, compound umbels terminate the main stalks and smaller ones originate in upper leaf axils. These plants sometimes form dense patches on choice sites. They bloom in summer. HABITAT: Moist ground or deep, well-drained soil from low to subalpine elevations. RANGE: Widespread and common in North America and Asia.

Parsley Family *(Apiaceae)*

Parsley Family *(Apiaceae)*

CANBY'S DESERT PARSLEY

Lomatium canbyi. The petals of many tiny, white flowers open just enough to contrast attractively with their purple anthers. Arranged in compound umbels, the umbellate rays are decidedly unequal in length. One or more leafless floral stems rise 4 to 8 inches from a taproot crown. Underground the taproot expands into a globe-shaped edible tuber to 1 1/2 inches in diameter. Smooth basal leaves divide into a multitude of small, rounded segments. This one blooms early in spring. HABITAT: Rocky prairies and hills, often with sagebrush. RANGE: Eastern Washington and Oregon and adjacent Idaho to N California. COMMENT: *Lomatium*, a genus found only in W North America, has about 75 species, many of them very difficult to differentiate. We have about 40 species of *Lomatium* in the Northwest, mostly frequenting the drier regions.

COUSE, COUS

Lomatium cous. In the early days Indians prized this species for food. The root expands into a globe or irregularly eggshaped tuber, encased in a brown husk. Native Americans ate the starchy tubers raw, cooked or dried and pulverized into flour and baked as bread. Lewis and Clark bought large quantities of bread made from "cows." Masses of tiny, yellow or sometimes purplish flowers bloom in compound umbels, the rays of the umbels unequal in length. The extremely variable leaves generally dissect two or three times into many short, crowded segments. Most if not all leaves originate on the root crown. Look for couse early in the season to midsummer, depending on elevation. HABITAT: Dry rocky plains and foothills into the mountains. RANGE: Central Oregon to E Montana, Wyoming and N Nevada.

Parsley Family *(Apiaceae)*

COLUMBIA DESERT PARSLEY

Lomatium columbianum. This unusual desert parsley displays several large pale to dark mauve umbels composed of many tiny flowers. The rays of the umbels all reach about the same length. The flower stems and leaves originate from a strong, woody taproot crown. A multitude of smooth, narrow, lacy leaf segments carry a delicate, bluish, glaucous coating. These handsome plants bloom early in spring. HABITAT: Rocky canyon walls and foothills. RANGE: The eastern portion of the Columbia Gorge and north along the E slope of the Cascades to central Washington.

GRAY'S (PUNGENT) DESERT PARSLEY

Lomatium grayi. The strong, distinctive odor, unpleasant when crushed to quite pleasant on balmy spring breezes, readily identifies this species of desert parsley. The leaves and bare flower stems attach to a branching root crown and spread in a rather dense clump. The leaves divide innumerable times into narrow segments about 1/4 inch long. Numerous tiny, yellow flowers of the compound umbel form tight clusters up to 4 inches in diameter in the spring. HABITAT: Dry rocky slopes and meadows from low river bottoms to moderate altitude in the mountains. RANGE: Columbia Basin to Idaho, Utah and W Colorado.

Parsley Family *(Apiaceae)*

Parsley Family *(Apiaceae)*

BISCUITROOT

Lomatium macrocarpum. Another desert parsley with edible roots produces masses of tiny white or purplish flowers on compound umbels. One to several smooth stems reach 4 to 10 inches, unbranched below the umbels. The taproot grows quite thick and long. Many small, lacy segments dissect the leaves. They may be dark green, but often assume a rich gray tint. It blooms in spring. HABITAT: Open prairies and foothills. RANGE: East slope of the Cascades from British Columbia to Manitoba and south to central California, Utah and Wyoming.

Dogbane Family *(Apocynaceae)*

Ginseng Family *(Araliaceae)*

SPREADING DOGBANE

Apocynum androsaemifolium. These
pretty little bell-shaped flowers are
about 1/4 inch long, white to pink on
the outside and bright pink or red
striped inside. The flowers cluster on
branch ends and originate in uppermost
leaf axils. The oval leaves, smooth on
the margins and surfaces, tend to
droop. Milky sap characterizes these
plants that stand 1 to 2 feet tall. They
bloom in late spring and early summer.
HABITAT: Fairly deep, well-drained soil
in valleys to medium elevation in the
mountains. RANGE: Most of the United
States and Canada. COMMENT: Four
poorly defined species of dogbane
inhabit North America. The flowers of
all appear quite similar. Dogbane is
poisonous to livestock and can become
a pest to farmers.

DEVIL'S CLUB

Oplopanax horridum. Thick rambling
stems of this shrub, armed with fierce
yellow spines, grow 3 to 10 feet high
and tend to crook and twist. Attractive
maple-like leaves, 4 to 12 inches broad,
also carry smaller spines on the
peduncles and veins. A dense, spiky
raceme or panicle of small yellowish
white flowers crowns the stem and
bright red berries replace the flowers in
mid to late summer. HABITAT: Deep
wet woods and stream banks, usually
where western redcedar and hemlock
trees provide an overstory. RANGE:
Alaska to SW Oregon and east to W
Montana and N Idaho; also around the
Great Lakes and northward.
COMMENT: Anyone who has the
misfortune to encounter devil's club in
a brushy thicket will long remember
the unpleasant experience.

WILD GINGER

Asarum caudatum. In deep, moist woods this creeper makes solid ground cover with broad, heart-shaped leaves. Slender, hairy petioles hold the leaf blades 2 to 3 inches high and horizontal, so they hide the stems and flowers. The prostrate stems root at frequent nodes. The flowers usually bloom right at groundline on slender peduncles that originate in leaf axils. Three attractive, brownish-red or brownish-maroon sepals form a cup around the ovary at the base, flare broadly above and then taper to long pointed tails—1 1/2 to 3 inches. The flowers lack petals or they are greatly reduced, blooming from April to July. HABITAT: Shady forest, frequently in moist canyon bottoms. RANGE: British Columbia to central California from the Coast Range east to W Montana and the Blue Mountains.

Birthwort Family *(Aristolochiaceae)*

Milkweed Family (Asclepiadaceae)

SHOWY MILKWEED

Asclepias speciosa. Members of the milkweed family bear fascinating two-tiered flowers, the inflorescence an umbel. A five-pointed star of upward curving, hooded and hornlike stamens comprises the upper tier, while the lower tier consists of the petals, which hang downward. A pretty, bluish pink tinges the petals of showy milkweed. Pairs of coarse, lance-shaped leaves rest on short petioles. The plants grow 2 to 3 feet high, and spread from a strong underground root system. They bleed milky sap when injured. Blooms in summer. HABITAT: Moist places at lower elevations. RANGE: Western and central North America east of the Cascades.

Sunflower Family *(Asteraceae, Compositae)*   **Sunflower Family** *(Asteraceae)*

YARROW

Achillea millefolium. A flat-topped to somewhat rounded inflorescence typifies yarrow. Ordinarily white or sooty-colored, the flowers occasionally show pink or even yellow shades. An individual flower head, which looks like a single blossom, is usually composed of five ray florets and 10 to 30 disk florets. Each floret constitutes a complete flower. Quite rounded and about 1/8 inch long, a ray floret resembles a single petal. All members of the huge sunflower family have flowers composed of many such florets. Yarrow's leaf blades are dissected many times into narrow segments *(millefolium)*. These feathery, aromatic leaves attach mainly to stems that stand 1/2 to 2 feet tall. Soft, wooly hairs generously coat the foliage. The blossoms open from late spring into fall. HABITAT: One can find yarrow from the seashore to alpine heights and from open areas to fairly heavy woods, usually on poorer, well-drained soils. RANGE: Most of the N hemisphere. COMMENT: Steeping the leaves makes flavorful tea, said to have medicinal qualities.

ORANGE AGOSERIS

Agoseris aurantiaca. Relatively few wildflowers display orange-colored blossoms, so recognition of this burnt orange "false dandelion" comes easily. Only strap-shaped ray florets occur in the flowers, but the ones in the center of each floral head may resemble disc florets. In seed, the fruits bear feathery plumes to help them travel on the wind. The slender leaves grow from the base in a tuft, about half as tall as the flower stems and ordinarily show a few teeth on the margins. The blooms open in summer. HABITAT: Grassy slopes and meadows from high montane to alpine. RANGE: Western United States and across Canada. COMMENT: We also have several species of yellow-flowered *Agoseris* called mountain dandelion or false dandelion.

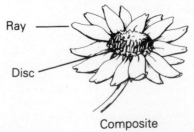

Ray ——

Disc ——

Composite

70

Sunflower Family *(Asteraceae)*

Sunflower Family *(Asteraceae)*

PEARLY EVERLASTING

Anaphalis margaritacea. Papery white bracts impart to these rounded clusters of stark white flowers their distinctive appearance. They lack ray florets. The plants stand 1 to 2 feet tall. Woolly, white hairs cover the narrow opposite leaves. The plant spreads from extensive underground roots. Blossoms appear in mid to late summer. HABITAT: Typically in forest openings. Pearly everlasting sometimes covers large clear-cut areas in the mountains soon after logging and provides valuable protection against erosion. RANGE: Much of mountainous North America, especially in the West, and in Asia. COMMENT: Makes excellent dried flower arrangements. It can easily be mistaken for several species of pussytoes.

DWARF PUSSYTOES

Antennaria dimorpha. Early in the growing season a low pussytoes, generally 1 to 4 inches high, greets the spring. Several stems spread along the ground from a root crown and send up numerous short branches. A compact head of white to greenish brown disc florets tops each stem. The flowers on each plant will be either male (staminate, as shown in the photo) or female (pistillate). The blossoms produce no ray florets. From the stems beneath the flowers, short, copiously hairy leaves create soft, silvery cushions. HABITAT: Grasslands, dry prairies and open spaces in the woods from low to moderate elevations. RANGE: British Columbia to Montana, Nebraska and California.

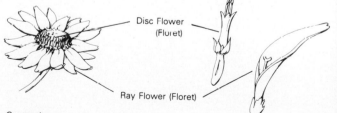

Disc Flower (Floret)

Ray Flower (Floret)

Composite

Sunflower Family *(Asteraceae)*

Sunflower Family *(Asteraceae)*

ROSE PUSSYTOES

Antennaria rosea. These pretty, little, white to pink or red floral heads lack ray florets. Papery bracts that surround the disc flowers carry the red coloration. The plant is mat-forming, spreading by stolons, which are aerial runners. They take root where they touch the ground. Dense gray hairs cover the stems and small spatula-shaped leaves. Rose pussytoes bloom from May to August. HABITAT: Open woods and forests to meadows and prairies. RANGE: Alaska and N Canada, south in the mountains to California and New Mexico.

ALPINE ARNICA

Arnica alpina. Yellow composite flowers, composed of both ray and disc florets, and opposite stem leaves identify *Arnica.* Alpine arnica usually spreads from underground rhizomes and sends up unbranching stems 2 to 8 inches high. A single flower tops each stem, which may have one to three pairs of stem leaves. Soft, matted, woolly hairs copiously coat the stems, leaves and floral bracts. Look for these bell-shaped beauties in midsummer. HABITAT: Rocky or gravelly alpine meadows, slopes and ridge tops. RANGE: The N hemisphere in arctic regions and high mountains, south to British Columbia and Montana.

HEARTLEAF ARNICA

Arnica cordifolia. Heartleaf arnica develops pretty, yellow, composite flowers on stems 6 to 20 inches high. Shallow notches scallop the ends of the ray petals. Two to four pairs of opposite, heart-shaped leaves attach to the stems and have irregular teeth on the margins. The plants spread from extensive underground roots, do not crowd themselves and many shoots bear leaves only. They bloom from April to June. HABITAT: Deep, coniferous forests and open woods from low to subalpine elevations. RANGE: The mountains of W North America. COMMENT: More than a dozen species of *Arnica* inhabit the Pacific Northwest.

Sunflower Family *(Asteraceae)*

Sunflower Family *(Asteraceae)*

BIG SAGEBRUSH, TALL SAGEBRUSH

Artemisia tridentata. Perhaps the plant that best symbolizes western America, at least the dry interior areas, is big sagebrush. Its gnarled, shrubby form and aromatic fragrance characterize the wide open spaces of the west. Short, white hairs impart a gray-green tint to the small, wedge-shaped leaves that display three small lobes at the tips. Stout, tough branches, covered with stringy, twisted bark, may stand 5 feet tall or more but only reach 1 foot on the harshest sites. The tiny, drab, yellow or brownish flower heads open in late summer. HABITAT: Dry open flats, scabland and foothills. RANGE: Much of W America. COMMENT: We have about 25 species of *Artemisia* in our region.

73

Sunflower Family *(Asteraceae)*

Sunflower Family *(Asteraceae)*

SHOWY ASTER

Aster conspicuus. A branching, somewhat flat-topped inflorescence of few to many blooms crowns a simple stem, 12 to 40 inches tall. The individual flower heads grow about 1 inch long with blue to lavender ray florets. Oval leaves, sessile, sharp-pointed and mostly toothed reach 2 to 7 inches long. The leaves on the lower stem are small and tend to wither and fall off early. Blooming occurs in late summer and early fall. HABITAT: Prefers open forest and margins from valleys into the mountains. RANGE: The Yukon and Saskatchewan to NE Oregon and Wyoming. COMMENT: One can easily confuse asters and daisies *(Erigeron)*. Asters generally grow tall and leafy stemmed, while daisies seldom possess these characteristics. The bracts below the flowering heads of asters develop in several rows of differing lengths and overlap like shingles, but daisies have one or two rows of bracts all about the same length.

LEAFY BRACTED ASTER

Aster foliaceus var. *apricus*. This admirable aster may have just one bloom or many blossoms in a branching floral arrangement. Leafy bracts subtend the rose, blue, lavender or purple flowers with yellow discs. The alpine variety shown here grows less than 10 inches tall, rising in a tuft of stems that curve at the base. Five other varieties mostly stand taller and grow at lower elevations. Sessile leaves clasp the stem while petioled leaves spring from the base. It blooms in summer. HABITAT: Moist ground in open woods or meadows at high montane to alpine sites; found at sea level in Alaska. RANGE: The Aleutians to California, Arizona and New Mexico.

Sunflower Family *(Asteraceae)*

ARROWLEAF BALSAMROOT

Balsamorhiza sagittata. The early spring sunflower of the Inland Empire and Northern Rockies, it grows in a clump from a large taproot that has a strong, bitter taste of balsam. Large leaves, shaped like arrowheads, are 10 inches long and 2 to 6 inches wide at the base, have smooth edges and are silvery gray with woolly hairs. The flower heads, 2 to 4 inches across, are solitary on long stems that overtop the leaves. Blooms in May and early June. HABITAT: Prefers well-drained soil on open slopes and foothills or open pine forest to near alpine. RANGE: British Columbia to the Black Hills and south to Colorado and California, east of the Cascade-Sierra summit. COMMENT: Most widely distributed and common of the balsamroots.

Sunflower Family *(Asteraceae)*

Sunflower Family *(Asteraceae)*

HOARY BALSAMROOT

Balsamorhiza incana. Hoary balsamroot usually develops two or more stems, 8 to 20 inches long, and displays a single flower head on each. The heads have about 13 or more yellow rays, 1 to 2 inches long. Silky, woolly hairs coat the involucre (the bracts beneath the floral heads) and, to a lesser extent, the leaves and stems. Note the buds in the photograph. Most of the leaves, 4 to 16 inches long, sprout from a thick taproot crown, but two smaller stem leaves usually clasp the stem base. Many pinnate leaflets cleave the leaves, have irregular teeth on the margins and often turn at right angles to the midrib so that they don't lie flat. Blooming from May to July. HABITAT: Dry foothills and lower mountains. RANGE: Blue Mountain region of Oregon and Washington to Montana and Wyoming.

TOOTHED BALSAMROOT

Balsamorhiza serrata. Toothed balsamroot differs from other members of the genus by always having some simple leaves with sharply toothed margins. In addition, the plants may often possess pinnately lobed leaves, the lobes also having teeth on the edges. Most of the leaves rise directly from the thick taproot crown and carry the blades on petioles, 1 to 5 inches long. The flower stems, which grow 4 to 16 inches long, may also support one pair of small leaves near the base. A single flower head tops each stem and expands 2 1/2 to 4 inches across. It blooms in spring. HABITAT: Dry rocky areas. RANGE: South-central Washington to NE California and N Nevada. COMMENT: We have six species of *Balsamorhiza* with toothed leaves in our region.

Sunflower Family *(Asteraceae)*

DUSTY MAIDEN, HOARY CHAENACTIS

Chaenactis douglasii. Several flower heads, white, creamy or pink, contain tubular disc flowers only and develop in a branching, flat-topped inflorescence, a corymb. The gray, hairy plants reach 4 to 24 inches tall and the stems may or may not branch. The leaves, 1 to 5 inches long and pinnately lobed, form a basal rosette as well as attach to the stem. Blooming can occur from late spring to the end of summer. HABITAT: Dry, often gravelly locations on prairies, foothills and into the mountains. RANGE: British Columbia to Montana, Arizona and California. COMMENT: Seven species of *Chaenactis* inhabit our region, several with small local ranges.

COMMON RABBITBRUSH

Chrysothamnus nauseosus. These bushy shrubs, from 1 to 6 feet high, brighten drab plains and deserts in late summer and fall, sometimes turning them golden. The growth habit varies considerably with a strong woody base but flexible twigs. The linear leaves alternate on the stems and bright yellow flowers have five to twenty blossoms per head. The flowers consist entirely of disc florets. HABITAT: Generally dry, open plains and foothills, often intermixed with sagebrush on poor, overgrazed or alkaline soil. RANGE: From Canada into Mexico, east of the Cascade-Sierras, to the Great Plains. COMMENT: Common rabbitbrush has six varieties and two other species of rabbitbrush occur in the Northwest.

Sunflower Family *(Asteraceae)* [Jack Strickler Photo]

Sunflower Family *(Asteraceae)*

ELK THISTLE

Cirsium foliosum. Elk thistle may grow as a low, tufted plant or with a single, edible stem to 3 feet tall that does not taper appreciably. The flowers vary from white to pink or nearly purple. Solitary flowers may occur, but more commonly, several flowers crowd the top of the stem. The leaves, pinnately toothed on the margins, develop short spines on the tips of the teeth. They bloom in late spring and summer. HABITAT: Open woods and meadows to alpine elevations. RANGE: Northern Canada to Arizona and west to the Cascade-Sierra summit. COMMENT: We have about 15 species of *Cirsium* in the Northwest, two of them introduced pests.

TAPERTIP HAWKSBEARD

Crepis modocensis. One or more stems per plant grow in a clump, 4 to 12 inches tall. Gray woolly hairs coat the pinnately lobed leaves, the lobes further toothed or lobed. Each stem may support up to nine narrow composite flower heads. Curly hairs as well as stiff bristles darken the involucres (the bracts of the composite blossoms). They appear from May to July. HABITAT: Dry sagebrush prairies and foothills. RANGE: Southern British Columbia to Montana, California and Colorado. COMMENT: Tapertip hawksbeard provides important forage for range stock, deer and antelope on sagebrush plains and desert areas.

Sunflower Family *(Asteraceae)*

Sunflower Family *(Asteraceae)*

DWARF HAWKSBEARD

Crepis nana. Many leaves and small, narrow flower heads create a tight clump, usually 4 inches high or less. Each blossom has about ten ray florets, but they reach only about 1/3 inch long, and minute teeth serrate the ray tips. The basal leaves, hairless and coated with a glaucous bloom, reach about as high as the flowers. Look for these charming little dwarfs in midsummer. HABITAT: Unstable scree slopes or gravelly or sandy areas at subalpine and alpine heights. RANGE: Asia and North America from arctic to high alpine regions, south to California and Utah in the west.

79

Sunflower Family *(Asteraceae)*

Sunflower Family *(Asteraceae)*

GOLD STARS

Crocidium multicaule. One or several stems *(multicaule)* of this small, fragile-appearing annual rise from a root crown, 6 to 12 inches high. A single yellow, composite flower head, about 1 inch across, crowns each stem. A rosette of basal leaves attaches with short petioles, while smaller, linear stem leaves grow alternate on the flower stems. A tuft of woolly, white hairs rests in the axil of each stem leaf. Gold star blooms usher in the spring. HABITAT: Prairies and other open spaces from low to moderate elevation. RANGE: British Columbia to California along the coast and western valleys and through the Columbia Gorge to South-central Washington and adjacent Oregon.

Axil

DWARF YELLOW FLEABANE

Erigeron chrysopsidis. From a tuft of linear leaves, less than 4 inches long, erupt several flower stems 2 to 6 inches tall. A single composite blossom, about 1 inch across, tops each stem. The stems and leaves normally wear sparse coats of short, straight hairs. Dwarf yellow flea-bane blooms from May into August, depending mainly on elevation. HABITAT: Prairies, often with sage-brush, to alpine heights in the Wallowa Mountains. RANGE: The Columbia Basin, Washington to N California and S Idaho. COMMENT: We have nearly 60 species of *Erigeron* in the Northwest.

Sunflower Family *(Asteraceae)*

Sunflower Family *(Asteraceae)*

CUSHION FLEABANE

Erigeron poliospermus. Cushion
fleabane produces many basal leaves 1
to 1 1/2 inches long, slender or
somewhat spatula-shaped and coated
with short, gland-tipped hairs. The
leaves thus make a low mat or cushion
on the ground. Floral stems reach 6
inches or less and usually bear just one
blossom, but occasionally the stems will
branch sparingly. The choice composite
flower heads radiate pink or lavender
rays around a yellow disc. This one
blooms in spring. HABITAT: Dry terrain,
often with sagebrush from flats to rocky
slopes. RANGE: Columbia Basin from
Cascades foothills to W Idaho and S
British Columbia to central Oregon.

SHOWY FLEABANE, OREGON DAISY

Erigeron speciosus. The name "showy"
suits this daisy or fleabane very well.
From a perennial taproot it sends up a
cluster of stems 6 to 30 inches high
and the stems normally branch from
upper leaf axils. A showy flower head
caps each branch end, spreading up to
150 narrow ray florets 2 inches across
or less. (Many narrow rays typify
members of *Erigeron*, whereas *Asters*
usually have fewer and wider rays, but
exceptions do occur). Blue to purple
rays usually beautify this one, but white
flowers show up on rare occasion.
Leaves assume narrow lance shapes
and grow smaller up the stem. It
blooms in summer. HABITAT: Moderate
elevations in woods and forest
openings. RANGE: Southern British
Columbia to the Black Hills, New
Mexico and Baja.

Sunflower Family *(Asteraceae)*

GAILLARDIA, BLANKET FLOWER

Gaillardia aristata. These large stately flowers display maroon to brownish discs and deep yellow to almost orange rays, three-lobed on the ends. The alternate leaves vary considerably, but usually reach 2 to 6 inches long and 1 inch wide. Look for *Gaillardia* in mid to late summer. HABITAT: Meadows and grassy prairies into the mountains. RANGE: Southern Canada, east of the Cascades, to Oregon, South Dakota and Colorado. COMMENT: A dozen native species of *Gaillardia* grow in W North America, but only this one graces the Pacific Northwest.

Sunflower Family *(Asteraceae)*

WOOLLY SUNFLOWER, OREGON SUNSHINE

Eriophyllum lanatum. This cheery little member of the sunflower family grows in a clump from a woody root. The stems may or may not branch and wear coats of soft, woolly hairs *(lanatum)*. A single flower, about 1 inch in diameter, terminates each stem or branch. The bright ray florets are often two-toned: yellow on the ends and orange toward the discs. Leaves, 1/2 to 3 inches long, sprout from the stems and can vary from linear to variously lobed, depending upon the variety. It blooms from May to August. HABITAT: Dry, open, grassy or rocky sites from low elevations into the mountains. RANGE: British Columbia to Montana and Wyoming, Utah and California.

COMMON (KANSAS) SUNFLOWER

Helianthus annuus. Our tallest annual and the state flower of Kansas, wild plants of common sunflower stand 2 to 7 feet tall, but improved, cultivated plants often grow much taller. The coarse stems and leaves wear stiff hairs that make them rough to the touch. They normally branch near the top, and each branch supports one large yellow flower, 3 to 5 inches across. Broad, alternate leaves are heart-shaped near the base and triangular above, tapering to sharp tips with small teeth on the edges. The floral centers are brownish yellow or reddish. As the common name implies, the flowers always face the sun, rotating from east to west each day. They bloom from mid to late summer. HABITAT: Open prairies and foothills, common on road edges. RANGE: Native to W United States; now widely cultivated for their oily seeds around the world.

Sunflower Family *(Asteraceae)*

83

Sunflower Family *(Asteraceae)*

Sunflower Family *(Asteraceae)*

SILVERBACK LUINA

Luina hypoleuca. Perhaps the outstanding feature of this strong perennial is its oval leaves, which present shiny, dark green surfaces above and white, densely woolly undersides. The clump of stems, 6 to 16 inches high, support all of the leaves and a similar coating of white, woolly hairs. Narrow, pale yellow, composite flower heads consist entirely of disc florets. The upper stems branch more or less irregularly into flat-topped inflorescences, composed of ten or more of the flower heads. Blooms appear in summer and early fall. HABITAT: Rocky slopes and cliffs. RANGE: The Cascades and Coast Ranges, British Columbia to central California.

BLACK-HAIRY MICROSERIS, FALSE DANDELION

Microseris nigrescens. A tuft of simple, narrow leaves with smooth margins and light center stripes sends up a single floral stem, 2 to 12 inches high. One flower composed entirely of ray florets terminates the stem. The under side of the floral head, called the involucre, is stippled with purple dots. In fruit the fluffy seeds resemble dandelions. The flowers bloom from May to July, depending upon elevation. HABITAT: Dry open meadows and slopes in the foothills and mountains. RANGE: Idaho, W Montana and N Wyoming. COMMENT: This species closely resembles Suksdorf's microseris, *M. troximoides,* which inhabits the Great Basin, east of the Cascades to W Montana, N Utah and N California and is sometimes classified with it as one species.

Sunflower Family *(Asteraceae)*

SWEET COLTSFOOT, FRIGID COLTSFOOT

Petasites frigidus. Several to many white or pinkish, cup-shaped heads stand erect upon an upright stem 4 to 20 inches tall. The floral heads usually contain all male (staminate) or female (pistillate) disc flowers. The stems bear a loose coating of alternate, parallel-veined and overlapping bracts. The leaves emerge after the flowers on long petioles from underground rhizomes. They bloom very early in the growing season. HABITAT: Wet or marshy ground in woods and often on roadside ditches. RANGE: Cold forest regions of the northern hemisphere, from the Cascades to the coast, south to S California, Michigan and Massachusetts. COMMENT: Arrowleaf coltsfoot, *P. sagittata*, a smaller plant, seems to bloom infrequently and much before the leaves emerge.

ARROWLEAF GROUNDSEL

Senecio triangularis. The names of this plant, both Latin and common, refer to the distinctive, triangular or heart-shaped leaves, which all grow along the full height of the stem. The larger leaves along the middle of the stem have quite long petioles, while the upper leaves are smaller and become sessile. Conspicuous, sharp teeth line the leaf margins. Most commonly the stems grow 2 to 4 feet tall, but one may also encounter taller plants. Few or many attractive, yellow to orangish flower heads occur in a branched, flat-topped inflorescence. Each head displays about eight ray florets, blooming through the summer. HABITAT: Common on wet or moist ground in forests and in open spaces usually from middle elevations to subalpine or lower alpine. RANGE: Western Canada and United States. COMMENT: A smaller, less common form of arrowleaf groundsel inhabits sphagnum bogs along our coast. More than 30 other species of *Senecio* reside in the Pacific Northwest.

Sunflower Family *(Asteraceae)*

Sunflower Family *(Asteraceae)*

DWARF ALPINE BUTTERWEED

Senecio resedifolius. This striking little plant bears one or occasionally two flowers on stems 2 to 6 inches high. The central disc may vary from yellow to orange or even reddish, and the yellow ray florets may reach 1/2 inch in length or even fail to appear entirely. Basal leaves are quite round or kidney-shaped, to 1 inch across, and may have rounded teeth or smooth edges. Smaller stem leaves grow sessile and have sharp teeth on the margins. They bloom in summer. HABITAT: Rocky alpine tundra or slopes in the high mountains. RANGE: Circumpolar in the N hemisphere, south to Washington and Montana.

Sunflower Family *(Asteraceae)*

Sunflower Family *(Asteraceae)*

CANADA (MEADOW) GOLDENROD

Solidago canadensis. Although many people blame goldenrod for their hayfever, other plants cause the summer malady more often than not. Canada goldenrod spreads by rhizomes and its stems may rise individually or in colonies about 1 to 4 feet tall or more. The stems, simple below, branch in the inflorescence and bear many small, composite flower heads of yellow ray florets. The branches usually curve outward and upward and sometimes tend to crowd just one side of the stem. All of the leaves grow on the stems and the small lowermost leaves usually dry up and fall off early in the season. The lance-shaped leaves have little or no leaf petiole and grow quite uniform in size on the upper stem. We have three varieties in the Pacific Northwest that bloom in summer and early fall. HABITAT: Dry sunny sites and open forests from the prairies into the mountains. RANGE: Alaska, most of Canada and the lower 48 and E Siberia. COMMENT: About a dozen species of goldenrod inhabit our region. Missouri goldenrod, *S. missouriensis*, could easily be mistaken for this one, but it has basal leaves and the floral branches usually turn downward.

NORTHERN GOLDENROD

Solidago multiradiata. Several yellow flower heads form somewhat flat-topped, branching floral sprays on low plants, 2 to 20 inches tall. Each composite head normally reveals about 13 or more ray florets. Basal leaves rest on distinct petioles, the ends nearly rounded or obtusely pointed. The floral stems originate from rhizomes and bear a coating of hairs, at least on the upper portion. Blooming occurs in midsummer. HABITAT: Mountainous terrain, subalpine and alpine. RANGE: Alaska and much of Canada, south to California and New Mexico. COMMENT: Alpine dune goldenrod, *S. spathulata*, a very similar species, usually shows fewer ray florets per head (about 8) and rounded, somewhat toothed leaves.

87

Sunflower Family *(Asteraceae)*

Sunflower Family *(Asteraceae)*

NORTHERN DUNE TANSY

Tanacetum douglasii. These coarse plants grow to 2 feet tall in leafy colonies from spreading rhizomes. Basal leaves may be present or lacking. All leaves, spatula-shaped in outline, divide pinnately two or three times into feathery, fernlike fronds with innumerable, tiny, rounded segments. They are aromatic and bright green. Twenty or fewer flower heads, about 1/2 inch across, form branching, flat-topped inflorescences. One usually does not notice the tiny ray florets as the plant blooms through the summer months. HABITAT: Coastal sand dunes. RANGE: Alaska to N California. COMMENT: Common tansy, *T. vulgare,* a taller alien species, has medicinal properties, but may become an invasive pest throughout our region.

PARRY'S TOWNSENDIA

Townsendia parryi. One or several stems rise from the base, each stem capped by one glorious bluish-purple flower, 1 1/2 to 3 inches wide. Parry's townsendia can grow as an annual, but more commonly as a biennial or short lived perennial. Narrow, lance-shaped or spatula-shaped leaves form a basal tuft, and a few smaller leaves cling to the stem. These plants bloom in late spring or early summer. HABITAT: High prairies and valleys to timberline. RANGE: Southwestern Alberta to Colorado and NE Oregon. COMMENT: Three species of *Townsendia* ornament our subalpine and alpine regions.

Sunflower Family *(Asteraceae)*   **Sunflower Family** *(Asteraceae)*

NORTHERN MULE'S EARS

Wyethia amplexicaulis This hardy
perennial features many resinous leaves
that appear varnished. The largest
leaves, up to 2 feet long and tapered on
both ends, sprout from the root crown
on short petioles, while smaller leaves
grow sessile on the flower stems. The
presence of sizable stem leaves
generally distinguishes mule's ears from
the balsamroots. One or several large
flowers top the stems that may reach 2
feet in length, but usually do not stand
upright. Look for these showy blooms in
May and June. HABITAT: Open prairie
with fairly deep soil to scattered timber
in the lower mountains. RANGE:
Eastern Washington to W Montana,
Colorado and Nevada. COMMENT: A
similar species, narrowleaf mule's ears,
W. angustifolia, generally ranges west of
the Cascades and lacks the shiny
leaves.

WHITE RAYED MULE'S EARS

Wyethia helianthoides. These white or
creamy flowers, 2 1/2 to 3 inches
across, sometimes turn pale yellow with
age. They grow in lush low clumps with
large elliptic basal leaves to 1 foot long,
usually smooth on the edges. Stem
leaves grow much smaller. The flowers
appear in May and June. HABITAT:
Moist meadows, woods and stream
banks at medium to subalpine
elevations. RANGE: Eastern Oregon to S
Montana, Wyoming and N Nevada.

Barberry Family *(Berberidaceae)*

VANILLA LEAF

Achlys triphylla. From a node on an underground rhizome rise two slender stems. The first one, a leaf petiole 1 foot tall or less, bears a single unique, three-bladed leaf *(triphylla)*, round in outline and up to 8 inches broad. Smooth, rounded scallops gracefully relieve the outer leaf borders. The second stem usually pokes up between two of the leaf blades as high as 16 inches. A dense spike of tiny white flowers, 1 or 2 inches tall, terminates the end of the flower stalk. The blossoms bristle with many stamens, but no petals, sepals or bracts appear. Numerous root nodes on a single plant can produce extensive colonies on favorable sites. Blooming occurs in spring. HABITAT: Deep, moist woods and forest openings. RANGE: Southern British Columbia to NW California, through the forests of W Washington and the W slope of the Cascades in Oregon. COMMENT: We have just the one species of *Achlys* in our region.

Barberry Family *(Berberidaceae)*

Barberry Family *(Berberidaceae)*

TALL OREGON GRAPE

Berberis aquifolium. The state flower of Oregon, this stout evergreen shrub normally stands 1 to 6 feet (or even 10 feet) tall. Five to eleven holly-like leaflets, arranged pinnately, compose a leaf, and numerous spiny prickles line the leaf margins. The older leaves may turn red or bronze after several years. Small, bright yellow flowers in several to many racemes form attractive clusters over the plant. Both sepals and petals, two-lobed at the tip, exhibit the yellow color. It commonly blooms through the spring. HABITAT: Open slopes and forests. RANGE: Southern British Columbia to W Oregon and N Idaho. COMMENT: Tall Oregon grape has been planted widely as an ornamental.

CASCADE OREGON GRAPE

Berberis nervosa. Cascade Oregon grape grows in a tight tuft of leaves and flowers and spreads by rhizomes. A low shrub, 1 to 2 feet tall, the leaves have more leaflets than the other species (11 to 21) and prominent, palmately spreading veins. The raceme of yellow, or sometimes red-tinged flowers, may reach 8 inches in length. It blooms through the spring. HABITAT: A forest species, from low to moderately high elevations. RANGE: Southern British Columbia to central California, from the W slope of the Cascades to the coast.

Barberry Family *(Berberidaceae)*

Borage Family *(Boraginaceae)*

NORTHERN INSIDE OUT FLOWER

Vancouveria hexandra. In forest shade dwells a dainty, white-flowering plant, the blossoms appearing to turn inside out. Six sepals and six shorter petals reflex sharply backward and then curl gracefully outward. Six yellow-tipped stamens tightly enclose a single pistil and form a cone-shaped nose for the flower. The blooms tend to hang downward in an open, sparsely branching inflorescence. The petioles of several leaves rise directly from the root, 4 to 12 inches, and branch two or three times. Broad leaflets have three or four distinctive, rounded ends. Look for this one from May to July. HABITAT: Coniferous forests and fringes. RANGE: West slope of the Cascades from Washington to NW California.

NORTHERN CRYPTANTHA, WHITE FORGET-ME-NOT

Cryptantha celosioides. A spike of white, open-faced flowers, about 1/4 inch in diameter, crowds the upper portion of a stem 4 to 20 inches tall. Several of these stems usually grow in a tuft on this biennial or short-lived perennial plant. The basal leaves broaden at the tip into spatula or oar shapes. A few smaller, narrow leaves attach along the stem. Dense white hairs, straight and somewhat stiff to silky, cover the leaves, stems and sepals. This one blooms in spring and early summer. HABITAT: Dry slopes and foothills into the lower mountains. RANGE: South-central British Columbia and Alberta to central Oregon, North Dakota and Nebraska. COMMENT: We have more than 20 species of *Cryptantha* in the Pacific Northwest. Most of them prefer dry, often sandy, slopes east of the Cascades. Only one resides west of the Cascade summit and one inhabits the alpine environment.

Borage Family *(Boraginaceae)*

Borage Family *(Boraginaceae)*

PACIFIC (GREAT) HOUNDSTONGUE

Cynoglossum grande. A branching cluster (a panicle) of dark blue flowers sits atop this rather coarse plant, 1 to 3 feet high. Five petals, fused at the base into a short tube, flare widely in an open-faced flower about 1/2 inch across. Sheer white petal scales in the throat give the blossom a pretty center "eye." In fruit four round nutlets, covered with hooked bristles, cling to clothing and animal fur. The leaves attach to the lower half of the stem. They all have long petioles and broadly lance-shaped or oval leaf blades, 3 to 8 inches long. March and April for this one. HABITAT: Prefers woods and forest fringes at low to moderate elevation. RANGE: Southern British Columbia to central California, west of the Cascades and through the Columbia Gorge. COMMENT: We have three species of *Cynoglossum*, including common houndstongue, *C. officinale*, a native of Europe, that has invaded much of N America.

FORGET-ME-NOT

Hackelia micrantha. Who can forget the gay little forget-me-nots? The round, blue, open-faced flowers become stick-tights that cling to one's clothing and animal fur in the fall. Perennial stems of this species branch from the base and in the inflorescence. Basal leaves and lower stem leaves are rough, hairy to the touch, narrowly elliptical, sharp-pointed and long-petioled. Upper stem leaves grow smaller and sessile on the stems. The flowers bloom from June to August. HABITAT: Lower mountains and foothills in open areas. RANGE: Southern British Columbia to Alberta, California and Utah; the Cascades eastward.

Borage Family *(Boraginaceae)*

HOWARD'S ALPINE FORGET-ME-NOT
Eritrichium howardii. One of the pure
delights for the high country explorer is
finding alpine forget-me-not. The indescribably blue flowers often completely cover the dense, long-lived
cushion plant. They may nestle among
the leaves, without noticeable floral
stems, or rise 3 or 4 inches high on
slender peduncles. Straight, silvery
hairs densely clothe the short leaves
that are less than 1 inch long. Blooming takes place in late spring and early
summer. HABITAT: High open prairies
and foothills to alpine mountain tops,
often on limestone substrate. RANGE:
Western Montana to the Bighorn
mountains of Wyoming. COMMENT:
One other species of alpine forget-me-
not, *Eritrichium aretioides*, also occurs
in the Pacific Northwest.

Borage Family *(Boraginaceae)*

Borage Family *(Boraginaceae)*

WESTERN GROMWELL, COLUMBIA PUCCOON

Lithospermum ruderale. This rough, sometimes weedy, plant branches freely from the base, making a clump 1 to 2 feet high. Many narrow, hairy leaves grow sessile on the stems, adding to the bushiness of the plant. From a bell-shaped tube, five pale yellow petals flare into an open face about 1/2 inch wide or less. These fragrant flowers also tend to crowd the stem ends, nestling among the many leaves, chiefly in late spring. HABITAT: Dry prairies and open timber at low to moderate elevations. RANGE: British Columbia to N California and Alberta to Colorado, mostly east of the Cascades; occasional around Puget Sound. COMMENT: Native Americans used the plant medicinally, including birth control.

TALL BLUEBELL

Mertensia paniculata. Tall bluebell usually grows as a tuft of stems, sometimes to 5 feet high but normally much shorter. Basal leaves, if present, sport long petioles, while upper stem leaves rest on short petioles. The leaf blades are thin, roundly heart-shaped at the base and lance-shaped or oval up the stem. The branching inflorescence, a cyme, displays an open cluster of pale to dark blue flowers, about 1/2 inch long, in which the bell (the outer portion) is somewhat longer than the tube. May to August depending on elevation. HABITAT: Moist ground in the mountains. RANGE: Alaska and much of Canada, south to Montana and SW Oregon. COMMENT: A very similar tall bluebell, *M. ciliata*, has flowers with bell and tube approximately the same length and sessile upper stem leaves. We have 11 species of *Mertensia* in the Pacific Northwest.

Borage Family *(Boraginaceae)*

Borage Family *(Boraginaceae)*

WOOD FORGET-ME-NOT, ALPINE FORGET-ME-NOT

Myosotis sylvatica var. *alpestris (Myosotis alpestris).* This lovely forget-me-not, the state flower of Alaska, grows in an upright spray of stems, 4 to 10 inches high. The stems may or may not branch. Yellow, red or white center eyes, sometimes all on the same plant, contrast brilliantly with five deep blue petals. Long soft hairs clothe the oblong leaves that erupt in a tuft from the base, and some smaller sessile leaves grace the flower stems. Blooms appear from late spring into summer. HABITAT: Meadows and grassy slopes from subalpine upward. RANGE: Circumboreal. In North America, Alaska to Idaho, Colorado and Utah. COMMENT: At least four genera of borages, *Cryptantha, Eritrichium, Hackelia* and *Myosotis,* are called forget-me-not.

RUSTY POPCORN FLOWER

Plagiobothrys nothofulvus. Small annual plants send up one or several stems 4 to 16 inches high. The stems may or may not branch sparingly. Narrow leaves less than 1 inch long form a tight basal rosette, and a few sessile leaves alternate on the stem. Short, stiff hairs make stems and leaves feel rough to the touch. A short raceme or spike of small, white flowers, about 1/4 to 1/3 inch across, terminates the stem. At first blooming in the spring the inflorescence curls in a "fiddleneck." HABITAT: Open prairieland. RANGE: The Columbia Gorge and Oregon Cascades. COMMENT: One can find eight similar species of popcorn flower in our region.

Mustard Family *(Brassicaceae, Cruciferae)*　　　　Mustard Family *(Brassicaceae)*

WALDO ROCKCRESS

Arabis aculeolata. Members of the
mustard family have four petals,
typically arranged in the shape of a
cross. This rockcress more commonly
shows an irregular pattern of petal
arrangement. The 1/2-inch long petals
are dark, reddish purple and rounded on
the ends. The inflorescence is a sparse
but rather crowded raceme. Several
slender stems, unbranched below the
flowers, rise 6 to 14 inches high. A
rosette of leaves 1/2 to 1 inch long,
entire or few-toothed, surround the
stems at the base. Linear to somewhat
oval leaves grow alternately on the
stems. They bloom in spring. HABITAT:
Dry, gravelly ground. RANGE: Endemic
to SW Oregon. COMMENT: We have
more than 20 species of *Arabis* in the
Northwest, many of them small and
weedy.

YELLOW WHITLOW GRASS, DRABA

Draba spp. No less than 11 species of
Draba are alpine mat-formers that send
short, woody branches radiating along
the ground. Short, mostly narrow leaves
overlap like shingles and add a cushion
effect to the plants. Rather short, naked
flower stems rise from the branches
and develop few-flowered racemes of
open-faced, 4-petaled flowers. The
distinguishing characters among the
species have mainly to do with the fruit
and types of hairs on the leaves. Two
species present white flowers and the
rest yellow. Blooming occurs mainly in
late spring and summer. HABITAT:
Mostly rocky alpine slopes. RANGE:
High mountains of the Pacific
Northwest.

Mustard Family *(Brassicaceae)*

Mustard Family *(Brassicaceae)*

DOUGLAS' WALLFLOWER

Erysimum capitatum. Considerable
confusion and disagreement seems to
exist among botanists concerning the
identification of various species of
wallflower. Some would probably lump
the present species with prairie
wallflower, *E. asperum*, which occurs
most commonly on the Great Plains.
The obvious teeth on the upper leaves
of the plant shown here differ, however,
from the entire leaves of *E. asperum*.
Furthermore, Sierra wallflower, *E.
perenne*, and Cascade wallflower, *E.
arenicola*, which may in reality be just
one species, differ from the present
plant in technical characteristics mostly
pertaining to the seed pods and seeds.
Such is the state of the art that makes
this author's work interesting if not
frustrating. Douglas' wallflower stands
1/2 to 3 feet tall, may or may not
branch and blooms through the spring
and early summer. HABITAT: Prairies,
foothills and dry rocky areas. RANGE:
Western America.

DAGGERPOD

Phoenicaulis cheiranthoides. One of the
early spring perennials, *Phoenicaulis*
has only this one species. From a
rosette of velvety, hairy, grayish green,
lance-shaped leaves, 1 1/2 to 6 inches
long, radiate several, usually prostrate,
floral stems. Numerous four-petaled
flowers, about 1/4 inch across the face,
crowd the stem ends. Petioles of
various length in the raceme create an
attractive, spreading, floral spray. The
flowers may vary from nearly white to
pink to deep magenta. Relatively long,
sharp-pointed seed pods give rise to
the common name. HABITAT: Sagebrush prairie to open forest from low
elevation to mountain ridges. RANGE:
East slope of the Washington Cascades
to Idaho, Nevada, the S Coast Range
and Sierras.

Mustard Family *(Brassicaceae)*

Mustard Family *(Brassicaceae)*

OREGON TWINPOD

Physaria oregana. From a perennial taproot, several or many stems spread prostrate, 2 to 8 inches, and turn up at the ends. A raceme of yellow flowers cluster at stem end and elongate somewhat in fruit. A basal rosette of leaves has rounded blades on fairly long petioles that may be simple or winged or lobed. Stem leaves are smaller and narrow. Stems, leaves and calyx all bear dense coats of starburst hairs that give them a gray-green cast and require magnification for fullest appreciation. In fruit the pods assume a flat, rounded heart shape. A spring bloomer.
HABITAT: Canyons and foothills. RANGE: Blue Mountains and adjacent Idaho.
COMMENT: In flower another species, *P. geyeri*, appears very similar, as well as several species of bladderpod, *Lesquerella*.

THICK-LEAVED THELYPODY

Thelypodium laciniatum. Tall, feathery plumes of white flowers, sometimes purplish at the base, ornament a cluster of branching stems, 1 to 8 feet long. The petals are very narrow, 1/4 to 3/4 inch, and help to create the feathery appearance. Rather fleshy or succulent leaves reach 4 to 18 inches in length. They have pinnately lobed blades with teeth on the margins in the variety shown. One may find the plants in bloom from April to July. HABITAT: Dry, rocky prairie or desert, often on basalt cliffs. RANGE: Columbia Basin and Great Basin.

Cactus Family *(Cactaceae)*

PLAINS PRICKLY PEAR

Opuntia polyacantha. Our most abundant cactus, plains prickly pear grows in clumps 6 to 12 inches high and has jointed stems. The pads and joints are both flattened. Slightly barbed spines 1 to 2 inches long arm the plants. The pads (stems) function as leaves, carrying out photosynthesis, since cacti have no leaves or lose them when young to prevent water loss. The succulent pads store water, and a waxy coating limits evaporation. The flowers, pale lemon yellow and waxy, sometimes display reddish tinges or bright red coloration.
HABITAT: Dry ground at low to mid elevations, often with sagebrush.
RANGE: Widespread east of the Cascades to Missouri and Mexico.
COMMENT: Three species of prickly pear occur in the Northwest. Cactus plants of all kinds have been collected for home and garden, and some species are threatened with extinction. Native wild cacti should be enjoyed in their natural habitat and left undisturbed.

Harebell Family *(Campanulaceae)*

PIPER'S BELLFLOWER, OLYMPIC BLUEBELL

Campanula piperi. This gem of Olympic National Park forms loose, low, spreading mats. Flower stems, 2 to 4 inches high, lift blue or occasionally white, 5-pointed stars to delight alpine visitors. At the floral base a short tube opens wide into a shallow saucer. The leaves occur both basally and on the stems, reach about 1 inch in length at the most, have sharp, serrate teeth on the margins and spread widest near the end. They bloom in midsummer. HABITAT: Rock crevices and benches at alpine heights. RANGE: Endemic to the Olympic mountains. COMMENT: Rough harebell, *C. scabrella,* produces similar flowers but bears entire instead of toothed leaves.

COMMON HAREBELL, BLUEBELLS OF SCOTLAND

Campanula rotundifolia. Common and widespread, this perennial varies considerably in its growth habit. While linear stem leaves predominate, the basal leaves on some plants are quite round, as the species' name implies. On others only linear leaves occur or the round ones wither early. Plants in the lowlands may grow 6 to 20 inches tall and bear numerous blue or somewhat lavender, bell-shaped and nodding flowers on threadlike pedicels. Dwarfed alpine specimens, 2 or 3 inches tall, may each support just one full-sized or oversized blossom. It blooms from late spring to the end of the growing season. HABITAT: Variable from low elevation to alpine, usually on dry, open or well-drained sites. RANGE: Hemispheric, south of arctic regions.

Harebell Family *(Campanulaceae)*

Harebell Family *(Campanulaceae)*

SCOULER'S HAREBELL

Campanula scouleri. Small, bell-shaped flowers, 1/3 to 1/2 inch in length, make few-flowered racemes on a weak perennial stem, 3 to 12 inches long. Five petals, tinted pale blue or lavender, curl gracefully backward and taper to sharp points. A single pistil projects noticeably out of the bell and presents a swollen stigma to view. The slender stems branch and often rely on grass or other plants for support. Leaves at the base are quite rounded and rest on long petioles. Progressively up the stem the leaves become narrower and pointed, eventually without a petiole. All leaves wear sharp teeth on the edges. Late spring to midsummer for this one. HABITAT: Retiring in woods but occasionally on open slopes. RANGE: Cascades to the coast, Alaska to California.

Caper Family *(Capparidaceae)*

Honeysuckle Family *(Caprifoliaceae)*

YELLOW BEE PLANT

Cleome lutea. This annual plant, 1 to 3 feet tall, branched or unbranched, bears a raceme of tightly crowded, yellow flowers at stem ends. The blooms have four bright yellow petals and six stamens that project well beyond the petals. Each blossom opens about 1 inch wide. Tubular seed capsules, 1/2 to 1 inch long, hang from slender pedicels that originate in the axils of mostly simple upper stem leaves or bracts. The inflorescence lengthens considerably as the capsules develop. Lower stem leaves spread five (three to seven) palmately divided leaflets, 1 to 2 inches long, narrow and rounded at the ends. Look for the flowers from May to July. HABITAT: Sandy ground from near desert to mountain valleys. RANGE: East slope of the Washington Cascades to Montana, New Mexico and E California. COMMENT: Another species, golden spiderflower, *C. platycarpa*, has boat-shaped seed capsules and ranges from central Oregon and S Idaho south in the Great Basin.

TWINFLOWER

Linnaea borealis. Slender, woody branches lie prostrate, often creating extensive carpets on the mossy forest floor. Short, leafy stems stand erect at frequent nodes, topped by pairs of dainty flowers on slender peduncles. The blossoms begin as narrow tubes but flare to five-pointed trumpets. They are white, pink or sometimes rose-colored and hairy within. They bloom in the summer. HABITAT: Commonly found in moist, dense forest to scattered woods. RANGE: The N hemisphere from polar regions south to California, New Mexico and West Virginia. COMMENT: One can easily introduce twinflower to moist, shady gardens. It spreads rapidly, providing attractive ground cover. Named for Carl Linnaeus, father of modern botanical taxonomy.

Honeysuckle Family *(Caprifoliaceae)*

CALIFORNIA HONEYSUCKLE
Lonicera hispidula. This honeysuckle can be variously hairy, sometimes with stiff hairs and sometimes smooth and hairless. The vines reach 6 to 18 feet long and climb into trees and shrubs or trail over rocky slopes. The pairs of opposite leaves, 1 to 3 inches long, have distinctive bracts at the base, called stipules, that join together to encircle the stem. At the end of the vine the pair of leaves fuse together to encircle the stem in a shallow cup. One to three flower stems (peduncles) originate in the axil of this terminal leaf pair and support two to five flowers each. A flower begins as a slender tube and widely flares two lips. The upper lip has four rounded lobes and the lower just one. Purplish-red colors the flowers outside, and yellow shows within. In fall the vines bear juicy, red berries. Summer blooming for this one. HABITAT: Forests to brush fields and open rocky slopes. RANGE: Southern British Columbia to California, west slope of the Cascades to the Coast Range.

ORANGE HONEYSUCKLE
Lonicera ciliosa. Bright orange trumpets cluster on the ends of woody, climbing vines. The leaves grow opposite and broadly oval, except that the pair of leaves just below the flowers fuse together at the base and completely encircle the stem. Often climbing to heights of 15 to 20 feet, the vines use trees, shrubs and fences for support. Red or orange berries develop in late summer. They are seedy, pulpy and edible, but not very tasty. Blooms from May to July. HABITAT: Deep forest to open woods at low to middle elevations in the mountains. RANGE: The Pacific coast to W Montana, S British Columbia to N California.

Honeysuckle Family *(Caprifoliaceae)*

BLACK TWINBERRY

Lonicera involucrata. A pair of fused, yellow, tubular flowers sits upon two pairs of sticky, leafy bracts that turn from green to purple with age. This shrub grows 3 to 6 feet high or more, and the elliptical leaves have pointed ends. The fruit consists of pairs of black, round berries, joined at the base and still subtended by the colorful bracts. Look for the blooms from April to July. HABITAT: Stream banks to moist woods from the coast to high montane. RANGE: Western North America from S Alaska to Mexico. Occasional in E Canada and NE United States. COMMENT: Black twinberry fruit is reported to be both edible and poisonous by different authors. The tempting appearance belies their bitter flavor.

Honeysuckle Family *(Caprifoliaceae)*

Honeysuckle Family *(Caprifoliaceae)*

RED TWINBERRY

Lonicera utahensis. A pleasing shrub, 2 to 6 feet tall, produces luxuriant, oval leaves. The cream or pale yellow blossoms, sometimes tinged with red, grow in pairs attached at the ovaries. The five petals unite in a tube about 1/2 inch long and flare prettily at the throat. A distinct spur, opposite the point of attachment, draws one's attention to the base of the floral tube. Red, watery berries join together in pairs and develop in mid to late summer. HABITAT: Scattered woods to fairly dense forest, at medium to subalpine elevations. RANGE: Southwestern Canada to N California, Wyoming and Utah.

Honeysuckle Family *(Caprifoliaceae)*

Honeysuckle Family *(Caprifoliaceae)*

BLACK ELDERBERRY, RED BERRIED ELDER

Sambucus racemosa. Conical or round-topped clusters, 3 to 6 inches across, of tiny, white flowers embellish a bushy shrub. The stem and twigs are thick but quite brittle and pithy. The pinnately compound leaves consist of five or seven lance-shaped leaflets with sharp teeth on the margins. The fruit develop into rounded masses of dark red or black, edible but seedy berries. A black-fruited variety (var. *melanocarpa)* occurs commonly in E Oregon and Washington and the N Rockies and the red variety (var. *arborescens)* from the Cascades to the coast. Flowers bloom from May to July. HABITAT: Moist woods and forest openings in the mountains. RANGE: Hemispheric, south in the mountains to New Mexico, Arizona and California. COMMENT: Blue elderberry, *S. cerulea,* bears flowers and fruit in flat-topped clusters. Home winemakers prize the berries.

Honeysuckle Family *(Caprifoliaceae)*

HIGHBUSH CRANBERRY, SQUASHBERRY

Viburnum edule. Clusters of small, white, tubular flowers, each about 1/4 inch wide, terminate short side branches above a single pair of opposite leaves. These shrubs grow 2 to 6 feet tall or more. The inflorescence, composed of 30 flowers or less, normally spreads 1 inch wide or a little more. Distinctive, palmately veined leaves, rounded at the base, extend three shallow, pointed lobes at the ends. The leaf margins show many sharp teeth and the leaves turn crimson in the fall. Juicy, orange-red fruit, edible but tart, have single flattened pits. The flowers appear from May to July. HABITAT: Stream banks and wet woods or bogs from low to fairly high elevations. RANGE: Alaska and much of Canada to the Oregon Cascades, W Montana and Colorado. COMMENT: We also have two other species of bush cranberry.

Honeysuckle Family *(Caprifoliaceae)*

Pink Family *(Caryophyllaceae)*

COMMON SNOWBERRY

Symphoricarpos albus. Common snowberry grows as a many-branched shrub, 2 to 6 feet tall, and spreads by strong underground rhizomes. Snowy white, waxy berries, occasionally lined with red, cluster on terminal twigs and afford the outstanding feature of the plants. The flowers, white or pinkish, 1/4 inch long or less, make tiny cups that wear a coat of fine hairs within. Short petioles support opposite pairs of oval or broadly lance-shaped leaves that may or may not have irregular teeth on the edges. The bloom peaks in early summer. HABITAT: A forest understory shrub to open areas from low to mid elevations. RANGE: Much of N America, south of arctic regions, south to California, Colorado and Virginia.

FRANKLIN'S SANDWORT

Arenaria franklinii. Franklin's sandwort forms a low-spreading cushion from a woody base. Numerous stems rise 1 or 2 inches from the supine branches. Many sharp, pointed leaves about 1/2 to 3/4 inch long overlap and provide a prickly mat below the crowded flower clusters at stem ends. Five sepals per blossom also show sharp tips and papery white margins. They are slightly longer than the small white petals. The plants bloom in late spring. HABITAT: Sand dunes or gravelly areas in scabland or ridges from low to quite high altitudes. RANGE: Central Washington to S Idaho and N Nevada. COMMENT: No less than 16 species of *Arenaria* enhance our region.

Pink Family *(Caryophyllaceae)*

MOSS CAMPION, MOSS PINK

Silene acaulis. Moss campion produces a thick, spreading mat up to 1 foot across. Gorgeous, five-petaled, deep rose to occasionally white flowers often literally cover the mats. Each flower crowns a stem, 1 to 2 inches tall. They grow tightly-packed from woody prostrate branches. The upright stems bear short, linear leaves that commonly remain on the stems for several years and add to the cushion effect of the plants. Summer for this one. HABITAT: Well-watered, rocky slopes and crevices in alpine terrain. RANGE: Circumpolar in arctic regions and south in high mountains to Oregon, Arizona and New Hampshire.

MOUNTAIN LOVER, MOUNTAIN BOX

Paxistima myrsinites. These dense low shrubs bear lustrous evergreen leaves about 1 inch long, sharpley toothed on the margins. Tiny, maroon, four-petaled flowers grow one or more in the axils of the sessile leaves. Look for these little jewels from May into June. HABITAT: Common at medium to lower levels in the mountains and woodlands, preferring open to moderately dense forest. RANGE: Southern British Columbia and Alberta, south to California and New Mexico. COMMENT: Mountain lover makes excellent low shrubbery plantings and Christmas greenery. It also provides important winter forage for game animals.

Stafftree Family *(Celastraceae)*

Morning Glory Family *(Convolvulaceae)*

BEACH MORNING GLORY

Convolvulus soldanella. Glorious light pink or slightly purplish, funnel-shaped flowers open 1 1/2 to 2 inches wide. White stripes reach from the pale yellowish center to the tips of the slight petal lobes. The flowers rise from fleshy, prostrate (not climbing) vines that may run to 2 feet long. Many succulent, shiny green leaves have distinctive kidney shapes. Flowering occurs from April to August. HABITAT: Coastal sand beaches and dunes. RANGE: British Columbia to S America, Pacific Islands (very common in New Zealand) and Europe. COMMENT: This morning glory, one of a half-dozen species in the Northwest, is not very common in our area.

BUNCHBERRY, DWARF CORNEL

Cornus canadensis. These low-spreading, perennial herbs make excellent ground cover. Four stylish white bracts, about 1 inch long, oval in outline and pointed on the ends, look like petals. These bracts in reality are specialized leaf scales. The minute flowers, arranged in a tight cluster in the center of the bracts, possess pretty purple accents. Larger than the bracts, bright green and the same general shape, the leaves form a whorl, four to six in number, below the blossoms. The fruit emerge in late summer as a bunch of small, red drupes that look like berries, edible but rather tasteless. Blooming occurs in June and July. HABITAT: Common in moist woods from low to mid elevations. RANGE: Asia and subarctic America, south to California, New Mexico and Pennsylvania.

cop. 2

Dogwood Family *(Cornaceae)*

Dogwood Family *(Cornaceae)*

RED OSIER DOGWOOD

Cornus stolonifera. These spreading shrubs often form thickets, 3 to 6 feet high. Bright red bark on stems and twigs attracts one's attention, especially in winter. The small flowers appear in a tight, flat-topped white cluster. The fruit develop into a bunch of bluish white, waxy drupes with single stones. It blooms mainly in June. HABITAT: Stream banks and other wet places from low, open sites into the woods and mountains. RANGE: Most of North America. COMMENT: Early pioneers used the inner bark as a substitute for tobacco.

111

Dogwood Family *(Cornaceae)*

FLOWERING DOGWOOD, PACIFIC DOGWOOD

Cornus nuttallii. Our most handsome flowering tree has been named the floral emblem of British Columbia. It sometimes attains a height of 50 to 60 feet, but more commonly reaches 20 to 30 feet. Its most beautiful display occurs in the spring when large, white or pinkish flowers, 3 to 5 inches across, simply clothe it. Some plants bloom again in early fall. Four to seven large, white bracts make a conspicuous blossom, surrounding a tight, rounded head of tiny green or purplish flowers.

Opposite leaves, oval in shape and 3 to 4 inches long, turn bright red in the fall. Clusters of red berries also add their color in the fall. Blooms occur from April to June and in September. HABITAT: Primarily a forest understory plant at lower elevations, but it can also prosper in the open. RANGE: British Columbia to California, west of the Cascade summit and disjunct in N Idaho. COMMENT: Flowering dogwood has been widely planted as an ornamental and can be grown from seed with overstory protection as a seedling.

Stonecrop Family *(Crassulaceae)*

KING'S CROWN, ROSEROOT

Sedum roseum. King's Crown generally does not exceed 6 inches in height. Tiny four-petaled, blood red to dark maroon flowers press tightly together in terminal heads and turn nearly black with age. The succulent leaves may have smooth, entire margins or show some scallops, as well as reddish-colored borders. It blooms from late spring to midsummer. HABITAT: Rocky or well-drained alpine areas, where moisture is available early in the season. RANGE: Circumpolar in the far north and south in the mountains to California, Colorado, Pennsylvania and Maine.

Stonecrop Family *(Crassulaceae)*

PACIFIC STONECROP, BROADLEAVED SEDUM

Sedum spathulifolium. The roots of this sedum seek nutrients and moisture in rock crevices. Tight rosettes of flattened, spatula-shaped leaves attach to sterile horizontal stems. A waxy, glaucous coating tints them a delicate gray color. Rounded, club-shaped stem leaves grow fleshy, succulent and alternate. They glisten with a waxy sheen on stems 3 to 8 inches high. On these upright stems sit flat-topped, branching clusters of yellow flowers in late spring and early summer. HABITAT: Moist cliffs or gravelly soil on or near the coastal region at low to moderate elevation. RANGE: Southern British Columbia to California, west of the Cascades.

BIGROOT, MANROOT, WILD CUCUMBER

Marah oreganus. From a thick, woody root grows a perennial, viny herb, 20 feet long or more, that climbs on trees or other available support or trails along the ground. Branched tendrils aid this strong climber. Large maple-like leaves have five or seven shallow lobes. Two kinds of flowers sprout from leaf axils. One readily notices the staminate (male) flowers that grow in a many-flowered raceme, but a single pistillate (female) flower sits below on a short peduncle. The white flowers typically spread five star-like petals from a small cup. The rounded, fleshy fruit, tapered on both ends and generally considered inedible, may or may not bear weak spines. HABITAT: Woods and low-lying open areas west of the Cascades from British Columbia to California and sporadic eastward along the Columbia river. COMMENT: Several other members of the cucumber family inhabit the west, but the only other one in the Pacific Northwest enters Montana and Idaho from the east.

Cucumber (Gourd) Family *(Cucurbitaceae)*

Oleaster Family *(Eleagnaceae)*

CANADA BUFFALO BERRY, SOAPBERRY

Shepherdia canadensis. This bushy shrub grows 3 to 12 feet tall and could be used for ornamental plantings. The simple, opposite leaves have greenish upper surfaces with noticeable veins. Gray or brownish scales speckle the hairy under-side of the leaves and small twigs. One can easily overlook the tiny, green or brownish, unisexual flowers in leaf axils, but the fruit become attractive yellow or red oval berries. They have a very bitter taste. Blooms early in the season. HABITAT: Deep woods to forest fringes or open areas. RANGE: Transcontinental; Oregon northward and eastward.

Heath or Wintergreen Family *(Ericaceae)*

CANDY STICK

Allotropa virgata. Bright pink or red longitudinal stripes decorate these exquisite, stark white spikes, 4 to 16 inches tall. The small, maroon flowers lack petals and nestle in the axils of pale leaflike scales. This plant is a saprophyte and blooms in summer, commonly following a soaking rain. HABITAT: Low to high montane forests. RANGE: Cascade-Sierra and Coast ranges from British Columbia to California and a disjunct population in the Bitterroot mountains of Montana and Idaho in lodgepole pine forests.

Heath Family *(Ericaceae)*

GREENLEAF MANZANITA

Arctostaphylos patula. This spreading evergreen shrub reaches 3 to 6 feet in height and has pretty, reddish bark. Pink, urn-shaped flowers, about 1/4 inch long, appear in branching clusters (panicles) on branch ends. The 1 to 2 inch long leaves, smooth and quite round or oblong, usually show a small point at the tip. They grow on rather short leaf petioles and may be green or somewhat yellowish. The flowers open early in the season, April to June, depending on elevation. HABITAT: Prefers open woods, often with ponderosa pine. RANGE: Southern Cascades to the California coast and east to Colorado.

Heath Family *(Ericaceae)*

KINNIKINNIK, BEARBERRY

Arctostaphylos uva-ursi. Small urn-shaped flowers, white to pink, bunch on the ends of branches of this prostrate shrub. The leaves are evergreen, waxy, smooth, oval and about 1 inch long. Edible red berries replace the flowers in mid to late summer, but they are pulpy and seedy. The flowers appear in late spring. HABITAT: Dense to open woods and forest edges. RANGE: Circumpolar in the N hemisphere. COMMENT: Two other species inhabit the Northwest. *A. columbiana* grows to 10 feet tall in the W Cascades and Coast ranges and *A. nevadensis* may stand 1 foot tall or resemble *uva-ursi* at high elevations of the Cascades, Sierras and Blue Mountains.

PIPSISSEWA, PRINCE'S PINE

Chimaphila umbellata. Five pink to rose petals open widely surrounding a prominent green ovary. Several of these charming, nodding flowers decorate stem ends. The plant is a low-spreading, evergreen semishrub. Leathery leaves, arranged in one or two whorls below the flowers, display small, sharp teeth on the margins. It blooms early in the summer. HABITAT: Coniferous woods where moist in the spring. RANGE: Temperate forests of the northern hemisphere, south to Colorado.

Heath Family *(Ericaceae)*

Heath Family *(Ericaceae)*

SALAL

Gaultheria shallon. One of our choice ornamental shrubs that can become invasive, salal usually reaches 1 to 4 feet tall. On the best sites, especially along the coast, it can grow much taller. It may stand upright or spread laterally. End branches about 8 inches long bear racemes of pinkish, urn-shaped flowers in leaf axils. The flowers and reddish twigs bear plentiful hairs, tipped with sticky glands. The oval leaves taper to sharp points and have small, sharp teeth on the margins. Dark purple or black berries develop in summer and fall. Indians collected them in large quantities, and birds and animals feed heavily on them. Blooms appear from May to July. HABITAT: Common in forests and open areas to moderate elevations. RANGE: West slope of the Cascades to the coast, British Columbia to California. COMMENT: Three other species of *Gaultheria* make low spreading ground cover.

Heath Family *(Ericaceae)*

Heath Family *(Ericaceae)*

AMERICAN PINESAP

Hypopitys monotropa. This saprophyte lacks green leaves and consequently lives on decayed organic matter in the soil. Unbranched stems, red to yellowish tinged, stand 10 inches high or less. The flowers nod and emerge from the axils of leaf-like scales, creating spiky racemes. They bloom from June to August. HABITAT: Forest duff from low elevation to subalpine heights. RANGE: Across North America and in Europe. COMMENT: Just one species occurs in our region, but several others are recognized in the E United States and Europe. Pinesap, though wide-ranging, is not very common.

WESTERN SWAMP LAUREL

Kalmia microphylla. The buds of swamp laurel present a fascinating study in design. A bright pink, closed cup shows ten prominent bumps where the anthers of the stamens rest in little pockets. When the flower opens, the anthers remain in the pockets until something jars the blossom. The stamens then whip upright, perhaps dusting an insect with pollen. These small shrubs, 8 to 20 inches tall, can spread vegetatively by layering or rooting where branches touch the ground. Opposite leaves, oval and 1/4 to 3/4 inches long, are green above and grayish below. They bloom from May through summer. HABITAT: Bogs and wet meadows mostly in the mountains. RANGE: Transcontinental in Canada and south to California and Colorado. COMMENT: A variety, *occidentalis*, ranges along the coast from Alaska to Oregon and produces narrow leaves, 1 to 1 1/2 inches long.

Heath Family *(Ericaceae)*

Heath Family *(Ericaceae)*

LABRADOR TEA, TRAPPER'S TEA

Rhododendron neoglandulosum (Ledum glandulosum). Sprawling, branching shrubs grow 2 to 6 feet tall and bear oval or oblong leaves. Dark green on the upper surface, the leaves show gray or white, hairy undersides. The edges of the leaves tend to roll under—much more on one coastal variety than on another that prefers mountainous terrain. Many white flowers crowd together in flat-topped clusters on stem ends. They bloom in early summer. HABITAT: Moist forests and thickets. RANGE: British Columbia and Alberta to Oregon and Wyoming. COMMENT: The original Labrador tea, *L. groenlandicum*, ranges across subarctic N America and south to the Oregon coast and N Idaho. It features a rusty coat of woolly hairs on the underside of its leaves. Early explorers supposedly used the dried leaves for making tea, but green leaves of both species are somewhat poisonous.

FOOL'S HUCKLEBERRY

Menziesia ferruginea. Yellowish, pink or bronze, urn-shaped flowers, about 1/4 inch long, grow in clusters of three or four at the ends of the previous year's growth. These shrubs stand 4 to 6 feet high and often make brushy understories in coniferous woods. The leaves are oval in outline, short-petioled and about 1 1/2 to 2 inches long, turning red or yellow in the autumn. They bloom from May to August. HABITAT: Moist woods from medium to subalpine reaches. RANGE: The Rocky Mountains from Canada to Wyoming and the Columbia River gorge. COMMENT: Another variety grows commonly along the Pacific Coast from Alaska to N California.

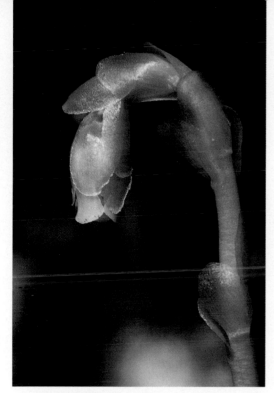

Heath Family *(Ericaccae)*

Heath Family *(Ericaceae)*

INDIAN PIPE

Monotropa uniflora. Waxy, white stems sprout in clumps, grow to 10 inches high and bear a single, pendent flower atop each stem. This saprophyte lacks green leaves and turns black and upright with age. The flowers appear in mid to late summer, usually following a soaking rain. HABITAT: Dense, moist woods. RANGE: Temperate North America. COMMENT: In years of plentiful summer rain, Indian pipe may be locally abundant.

RED HEATHER, PINK MOUNTAIN HEATH

Phyllodoce empetriformis. A low shrub spreads along the ground and branches profusely, frequently creating solid ground cover. The small, pink to rose, bell-shaped flowers cluster on branch ends and nod gracefully on slender, reddish, hairy pedicels. Pistils protrude from the bells but not the stamens. Needle-like, evergreen leaves densely cover the branches, reminding one of fir boughs. This exquisite floral display occurs in July and August. HABITAT: Moist alpine meadows and slopes. RANGE: Alaska and the Yukon, south in the mountains to California and Wyoming. COMMENT: Yellow mountain heather, *P. glanduliflora*, produces urn-shaped flowers and many sticky, gland-tipped hairs. White mountain heather, *Cassiope mertensiana*, has white, cup-shaped flowers.

Heath Family *(Ericaceae)*

Heath Family *(Ericaceae)*

PINEDROPS

Pterospora andromedea. This reddish or yellowish brown saprophyte lacks green leaves and lifts unbranched stalks 1 to 3 feet high. It lives on decayed organic matter in the forest floor. The flowers are about 1/2 inch long, urn-shaped or bell-shaped and numerous. They droop from slender pedicels in the axils of scaly bracts. Look for these unusual plants in the summer. HABITAT: Deep woods to open forests at low to moderate elevations. RANGE: Mountainous North America. COMMENT: Although pinedrops range widely, they seldom occur very abundantly.

PINK PYROLA, PINK WINTERGREEN

Pyrola asarifolia. Charming pink to rosy red flowers of pink pyrola are cup-shaped and generally tilt downward. A long, green style curves gracefully downward and out from each floral cup. The naked stalks reach 6 to 12 inches tall but carry an occasional scaly bract. The basal leaves, supported by long petioles, possess broad, green blades, 2 to 3 inches long. Pink pyrola seems to grow in symbiotic harmony with certain fungi in the soil and can therefore seldom be transplanted successfully. Blooms in summer. HABITAT: Deep woods, chiefly in moist valleys and on mountain sides. RANGE: Much of North America.

Heath Family *(Ericaceae)*

LEAFLESS PYROLA

Pyrola aphylla. No less than four species of pyrola, namely: white-veined pyrola, *P. picta*; pink pyrola, *P. asarifolia*; toothleaf pyrola, *P. dentata*; and greenish wintergreen, *P. chlorantha* may on occasion become parasitic on other plants by attachment of the roots. They then fail to produce green leaves and rely on the host plant for sustenance. Although they have no basal leaves in this form, 1 to 4 small stem bracts may possess some chlorophyll. Because leaf structure is diagnostic for identification among the numerous species of *Pyrola*, in the leafless plants one cannot be certain of identity. The name "leafless" *(aphylla)* is therefore applied to all 4 species. In general the plants branch at the base underground and send up several reddish brown stems 2 to 8 inches. Ten or more flowers 1/3 to 1/2 inch in diameter form a rather loose raceme, arising in the axils of tiny bracts. They may display white, greenish, pink or brown coloration or some combination of these, usually in midsummer. HABITAT: Coniferous forests. RANGE: British Columbia to Montana and California.

Heath Family *(Ericaceae)*

Heath Family *(Ericaceae)*

ONE SIDED (SIDE FLOWERED) PYROLA

Pyrola secunda. A shy recluse of the forest, this small plant nevertheless forms quite extensive colonies by spreading from underground rhizomes. Unbranched stems, commonly bent or nodding, reach 2 to 6 inches in length. Six to twenty flowers, white or greenish, all hang on one side of the stem. From each small, cupped flower, about 1/4 inch across, projects a single, straight style. Most other species of pyrola have exserted styles that show curvature distinctly. Several round or oval leaves attach to the lower stem. This one blooms in the summer. HABITAT: Moist coniferous woods. RANGE: Throughout much of the N hemisphere.

WOOD NYMPH

Pyrola (Moneses) uniflora. One may easily overlook these shy, little, waxy, white flowers, because the solitary blossoms usually nod. The five petals open wide from beneath a prominent green ovary. Wood nymph stands 1 1/2 to 6 inches tall, rising from one or two whorls of green leaves, usually three in number, near the base. It blooms in summer. HABITAT: Most common in wet areas in deep woods, but also on moist slopes near or above timberline. RANGE: Alaska to California and east to the NE United States. COMMENT: Distinctive and easily recognized, but not very abundant.

Heath Family *(Ericaceae)*

PACIFIC RHODODENDRON

Rhododendron macrophyllum. Surely the title of "Most Magnificent Flowering Shrub" in the Northwest must apply to pacific rhododendron. Washington has selected it as its state flower. Whorls of large, leathery, oval leaves, 4 to 8 inches long, evergreen and entire on the edges, frame a tight cluster of pink to deep rose flowers on branch ends. Individual blossoms begin at the base as funnel-shaped tubes and flare five gorgeous petals with crinkled margins 2 inches wide. An upper petal bears pretty brown speckles and the floral throat usually flashes yellow. A cluster may span 6 inches, and plants in preferred sites create solid masses of color 3 to 15 feet high from April to July, depending on elevation. HABITAT: Open to dense woods, commonly forming an understory from low to high elevations on acid soils. RANGE: West slope of the Cascades to the coast, British Columbia to N California. COMMENT: Worldwide, several hundred species of rhododendron have been identified and many have been introduced to the Northwest as ornamental shrubs. Our native species should never be dug for transplanting.

Heath Family *(Ericaceae)*

WESTERN AZALEA

Rhododendron occidentale. Lighter colored than pacific rhododendron, but spectacular in its own right, western azalea has some similarities to the former but also some important differences. The slightly irregular, fragrant blossoms start from narrow tubes about 1 inch long and may vary from white to pink or salmon. An upper petal displays a distinct yellow or orange patch or stripe. The leaves are shorter than pacific rhododendron, 2 to 3 1/2 inches, and they fall off in winter (deciduous). Look for this one from April to August. HABITAT: Moist slopes under some shade. RANGE: The coastal mountains from SW Oregon to S California.

Heath Family *(Ericaceae)*

SNOW PLANT

Sarcodes sanguinea. This spectacular, all red plant can be mistaken for no other and, once seen, cannot be forgotten. Its fleshy, unbranched stalks reach 4 to 16 inches tall and the bright red, overlapping bracts or scales are residual leaf-forms. However, the plant has no chlorophyll and therefore does not produce its own sustenance. It is a saprophyte, gaining nourishment from decayed organic matter in the forest floor. Cup- or slightly urn-shaped flowers, 1/2 to 3/4 inch long, sit in the axils of the upper bracts, forming a spikelike raceme. They all possess five well-rounded petals and bloom from April to July, soon after snow melt. HABITAT: Coniferous forest duff from moderate to high elevations. RANGE: Southwestern Oregon to California and Nevada.

Heath Family *(Ericaceae)*

Pea Family *(Fabaceae, Leguminosae)*

GLOBE HUCKLEBERRY, BLUE HUCKLEBERRY

Vaccinium globulare. Branching shrubs, 1 to 4 feet high, bear oval leaves about 1 to 2 inches long with very fine teeth on the margins. The branches are yellow (in new growth) to grayish brown. Small, drooping flowers are roundly urn-shaped and pinkish white. The blue berries have a light gray, glaucous coating and a delicious tart flavor. Huckleberries bloom in May and June and the berries ripen in mid to late summer. HABITAT: Forests and open mountain sides from low to mid elevations. RANGE: Eastern Washington to Montana and Wyoming.

BASALT MILKVETCH

Astragalus filipes. Basalt milkvetch sends up numerous stems in a clump, 1 to 3 feet high. Leaves erupt from lower stem nodes and produce 9 to 25 linear leaflets, or the leaflets may broaden near the tips. Floral stems originate in the upper leaf axils and reach well above the leaves. Open racemes of cream or pale yellow flowers tend to droop from the peduncles. The calyces bear fine coats of blackish hairs. The banner petals reflex, and the shorter, rounded wing petals mostly hide the keels in May and June. HABITAT: Sagebrush flats, foothills and canyons. RANGE: Columbia Basin to S Idaho, central Nevada and NE California; also disjunct in S California and Baja.

Heath Family *(Ericaceae)*

EVERGREEN HUCKLEBERRY

Vaccinium ovatum. The tallest of our huckleberry shrubs, 2 to 12 feet, grows in clumps, either spreading or upright, and branches profusely. Evergreen, leathery leaves, 1 to 2 inches long, tend to align in one horizontal plane on the branches. Small, sharp teeth serrate the leaf edges. The small, bell-shaped blossoms, White to pink, are supported by bright red calyces. They form few-flowered sprays near branch ends in late spring and early summer. HABITAT: Shrubby thickets. RANGE: British Columbia to California from the coast to the west slope of the Cascades. COMMENT: Black or bluish berries, sweet and juicy, appear in autumn.

Pea Family *(Fabaceae, Leguminosae)*

HAIRY MILKVETCH

Astragalus inflexus. Hairy milkvetch or locoweed grows in mats or upright tufts, 4 to 20 inches high, from a perennial taproot. Flowers and leaves generally reach about the same height. Six or more rose-purple flowers form a tightly clustered raceme on a leafless, unbranched stem. Hairs grow on the back of the banner petal, which bends noticeably backward. Rather dense hairs give the 15 to 29 oval leaflets on each leaf a grayish green color. Blooms April to July. HABITAT: Dry hills and sagebrush prairies. RANGE: Central Washington and Oregon to W Montana.

Pea Family *(Fabaceae)*

PURSH'S MILKVETCH, LOCOWEED OR SHEEPPOD

Astragalus purshii. This small sprawling plant grows in a rather dense tuft or mat. The stems only reach about 4 inches in length. Ten or fewer blossoms cluster at stem ends. They may vary from cream to magenta through no less than six varieties. Numerous pinnately compound leaves are grayish green from a covering of silvery hairs and may have from 7 to 19 oval leaflets. In fruit the pods, 1 inch long or less, literally disappear under woolly, white hairs. Spring or early summer. HABITAT: From sagebrush prairies into the mountains. RANGE: W North America, east of the Cascades.

Pea Family *(Fabaceae)*

COLUMBIA MILKVETCH

Astragalus succumbens. Pale blue to lavender striping on a white background, shading to solid lilac at the base, marks the banner and wing petals of these captivating blooms. A darker hue accents the tip of the retiring keel petal. From 10 to 60 blossoms affix to the floral stems in a raceme. Each blossom reaches about 1 inch in length. The stem and leaves carry a dense coat of silvery gray hairs. Several branching stems mostly recline outward from a stout perennial taproot. Each pinnately compound leaf has 13 or more oval leaflets. Columbia milkvetch blooms in mid to late spring. HABITAT: Sand dunes, scabland and foothills. RANGE: Central Washington to N central Oregon. COMMENT: In the Northwest we have a bewildering array of about 85 species of *Astragalus*, mostly on dry or near desert sites. Some, but not all, species selectively concentrate selenium from the soil in their tissues, which will poison animals and cause blind staggers or death if consumed in quantity. These species are often called locoweeds or crazyweeds. Also see *Oxytropis*, pp. 136-137.

SCOTCH (SCOT'S) BROOM
Cytisus scoparius. When foreign plants are introduced into an area, sometimes the lack of normal biological restraints in the new environment allows the alien to run wild and push out many if not all native plants. Scotch broom has thus invaded portions of our Pacific Coast, especially along the ocean front. Only established forests and the persistent hand of man seem to daunt its steady expansion. These shrubs reach 6 to 10 feet high, branching profusely with slender, greenish, square limbs. The yellow pea flowers grow one or sometimes more in leaf axils and literally cover the branches. In full bloom they make solid masses of golden color in the spring. Occasionally, the wing petals on a plant will assume a gorgeous dark red or purple shade. The leaves grow much smaller than the flowers, mostly in threes but single near stem ends. HABITAT: Roadsides and unused open areas. RANGE: British Columbia to California, west of the Cascades; the Old World. COMMENT: Gorse, *Ulex europaeus*, another invasive pest appears similar, but it develops fierce spines and makes impenetrable thickets.

Pea Family *(Fabaceae)*

Pea Family *(Fabaceae)*

SCOTCH (SCOT'S) BROOM
Cytisus scoparius.

Pea Family *(Fabaceae)*

NORTHERN SWEETVETCH

Hedysarum boreale. Numerous branching stems create a tufted perennial 1 to 2 feet high. Gaudy, upright or spreading racemes of five to fifteen pink to deep magenta or carmine flowers terminate stem ends. Typical of sweetvetches, the keel petal projects out much farther than the wings. In fruit a flat loment develops cross sections between its two to five seeds. The leaves have nine to fifteen oval- or lance-shaped and entire leaflets, 1/2 to 1 inch long. June or July for this one. HABITAT: Forest openings and high prairies. RANGE: Much of arctic North America, south to E Oregon and through the Rockies.

WESTERN SWEETVETCH

Hedysarum occidentale. Racemes of pink or dark magenta flowers adorn the upper ends of upright stems and droop, at least in the lower portion of the inflorescences. Keel petals considerably exceed banners and wings. Leaves start from nodes along the stem and have 9 to 21 oval leaflets, 1/2 to 1 inch long. The blooms can persist from June into September. HABITAT: Open woods and grassy slopes both above and below treeline. RANGE: Olympics and Cascades of Washington to Montana and Colorado. COMMENT: Alpine Sweetvetch, *H. alpinum*, produces similar or paler colored flowers in high mountains of British Columbia, Alberta and NW Montana.

Pea Family *(Fabaceae)*

133

Pea Family *(Fabaceae)*

Pea Family *(Fabaceae)*

BEACH PEA

Lathyrus japonicus. Tough, robust pea vines to 5 feet long, climbing or prostrate, invest sand dunes along the seashore. Adapted to the seaside environment, the stout, spreading rhizomes help prevent sand dune movement and beach erosion. Glorious wild sweetpeas vary from sky blue to purple in two- to eight-flowered racemes. Wing and keel petals generally assume lighter tones than the large reflexed banner. Pinnately compound leaves develop six to twelve oval leaflets and twining tendrils on the end help the vines climb if support is present. Two stipules, as large as the leaflets, subtend each leaf. Both leaves and stems are smooth, green and somewhat succulent. HABITAT-RANGE: Coastlines of the N Hemisphere and around the Great Lakes.

FEW FLOWERED PEAVINE, WILD SWEETPEA

Lathyrus pauciflorus. This captivating perennial sweetpea produces upright stems 2 feet tall or less. The pinnate leaves ordinarily have eight to ten leaflets and the leaf axes end in curling, branching tendrils. The leaflets vary considerably with the variety. Four to seven-flowered racemes compose the inflorescences and vary from pink to purple, turning blue with age. Blooms in mid to late spring. HABITAT: Medium dense forest to open prairies. RANGE: Eastern Washington and Idaho, south to W Colorado, NE Arizona and California.

Pea Family *(Fabaceae)*

PRAIRIE LUPINE
Lupinus lepidus. Generally low and spreading, prairie lupine sometimes makes cushions. The floral stems, 4 to 10 inches or more, may nestle among the leaves or project well above. Palmately compound leaves produce five to nine leaflets. Most leaves sprout from the base but some also originate on the stems. Leaves, stems and calyces all wear copious hairy coats. Numerous blue or sometimes white flowers crowd the upper stems with whorls of bloom. The banner petals bend sharply backward and are usually a different color from the wings and keels—either lighter (white) or darker. The plants bloom from June to August. HABITAT: Open prairie into the mountains. RANGE: British Columbia to Montana, Colorado and California. COMMENT: Although this species is fairly distinct from about two dozen other lupines, five varieties of prairie lupine in the Northwest create considerable differences within the species.

Pea Family *(Fabaceae)*

SEACOAST LUPINE
Lupinus littoralis. Coarse plants with branching stems up to 2 feet long lie prostrate at the base and turn upright on the ends. The dense mats of stems and leaves can cover large areas in favorable locations. Leaflets, 1 to 1 1/2 inches long, number five to nine, are widest near the end and have a tiny spine at the tip. The racemes of flowers grow in loose whorls, the purple wing and keel petals contrasting beautifully with the pale or white banners. Blooming can occur from late April until August. HABITAT: Flats and banks along the seashore. RANGE: British Columbia to California.

Pea Family *(Fabaceae)*

Pea Family *(Fabaceae)*

SULPHUR LUPINE

Lupinus sulphureus. As the names imply, sulphur lupine normally assumes a yellow color. However, a couple of varieties may be blue, probably through the tendency of this species to hybridize with other lupines. Several to many unbranched stems grow 1 1/2 to 3 feet tall. Typically many small flowers (for lupines), about 1/2 inch long, grace the upper stems, but usually do not crowd each other. The banner petal does not reflex sharply from wing and keel, but considerable variation can occur. Blooming time is April to June. HABITAT: Sagebrush plains to open mountain slopes and scattered forest. RANGE: South-central British Columbia to Idaho, the Willamette Valley and California.

SHOWY CRAZYWEED

Oxytropis splendens. Another species of crazyweed has densely hairy but soft foliage. The leaves grow 4 to 10 inches long and produce many leaflets in whorls of three to six per node. Closely packed spikes of purple pea flowers reach 2 to 4 inches high on floral stems that rise above the leaves. This is a summertime bloomer. HABITAT: Gravelly areas, meadows and road edges, in valleys and lower mountains. RANGE: Alaska to New Mexico in the Rockies and east to Ontario.

Pea Family *(Fabaceae)*

INFLATED CRAZYWEED

Oxytropis podocarpa. The common name of this oxytrope comes from the much-inflated pods, mottled green and purple and 1 to 1 1/2 inches long with pointed tips. One to three, but usually two, purple flowers with white in the throat affix to a short peduncle. The plants grow 1 or 2 inches high in a cushion—the small leaves bear nine to twenty-seven very short, narrow leaflets. Stiff silvery hairs coat the foliage. Blooming occurs in summer. HABITAT: Exposed, rocky, alpine ridges and slopes. RANGE: The Rockies and east across Canada. COMMENT: The crazyweed genus, *Oxytropis*, can be readily differentiated from locoweeds, *Astragalus*, by the presence of a small beak or point on the end of the keel petal. Some members of both genera have the facility to accumulate selenium from the soil in their tissues, which may poison animals, giving them the "staggers." If consumed in quantity, these plants can prove fatal to large animals.

137

Pea Family *(Fabaceae)*

Pea Family *(Fabaceae)*

WESTERN PRAIRIE CLOVER

Petalostemon ornatum Several stems that branch sparingly rise 1 to 2 feet from a woody, perennial root crown. Dense spikes, 1 to 3 inches long, of tiny pink or magenta to deep rose blooms adorn the stem ends. Before the flowers open, the buds or sepals usually wear a noticeable coating of soft hairs. The rest of the plant is quite hairless. Pinnate leaves with seven rather broad, smooth leaflets, attach alternately to the stems. Look for this one from May to July. HABITAT: Dry, open, rocky or sandy places, often with sagebrush or juniper. RANGE: The Columbia Basin of Washington and Oregon to S Idaho. COMMENT: Purple prairie clover, *P. purpureum*, and white prairie clover, *P. candidum*, reach the eastern base of the Rockies from the Great Plains.

GOLDEN PEA, MOUNTAIN THERMOPSIS

Thermopsis montana. These attractive clumps of bright yellow pea flowers, about 1 inch long, create elongated racemes from late spring to mid-summer. The plants spread from a strong underground root system, sending up hollow stems 2 to 3 feet tall. Three smooth narrow leaflets constitute a leaf. HABITAT: Variable, from low meadows to moderate heights in the mountains. RANGE: British Columbia to Montana and south to California and Colorado.

Pea Family *(Fabaceae)*

BIGHEADED CLOVER

Trifolium macrocephalum. Quite the largest and one of the prettiest of the clovers, the elegant flower heads expand about 2 inches in diameter. The pinkish white to rose-red blooms crown branch ends. The small, low plants may lie prostrate on open, uncrowded sites, but stand more or less upright when crowded. Five to seven leaflets normally make up a leaf, which is unusual for a clover. *Trifolium* means three-leaved. Bigheaded clover blooms in spring. HABITAT: Dry sagebrush plains to high gravelly ridge tops and scattered ponderosa pine forest. RANGE: East slope of the Cascades in Washington to Idaho and Nevada.

Pea Family *(Fabaceae)*

Pea Family *(Fabaceae)*

SPRINGBANK CLOVER

Trifolium wormskjoldii. Springbank clover produces three-bladed leaves, typical of most clover species. The leaves have tiny teeth on the margins, tipped with minute spines. Toothed and spiny bracts, called stipules, attach at the base of the leaves. Both leaves and stipules often are quite purple. The compact flower heads reach 1/2 to 1 inch across and may vary from white to lavender or deep purple. The banner may also reflect lighter tones than wing and keel petals. From creeping roots, prostrate and branching stems grow 4 to 30 inches long. The blossoms may persist from May into autumn. HABITAT: Wet ground from the coast, where it is quite abundant, into the mountains. RANGE: British Columbia to Mexico, Idaho and Colorado.

AMERICAN VETCH

Vicia americana. Four or more pretty purple or violet pea-like flowers grow in racemes from leaf axils. A perennial herb, 6 to 30 inches tall, the weak stems often recline. The leaves are pinnately compound and the ends of the leaves elongate to tendrils that may or may not branch and curl. American vetch varies in the shape of the leaves and presence or absence of hairs through three varieties. They bloom from May to July. HABITAT: Open fields and prairies, preferring fairly deep soil. RANGE: Most of North America. COMMENT: Several other vetches occur in the region, most of them native to Europe and Asia.

Bleeding Heart Family *(Fumariaceae)*

Bleeding Heart Family *(Fumariaceac)*

WESTERN CORYDALIS

Corydalis scouleri. This beautiful plant forms colonies from rhizomes and sends up hollow stems two to four feet tall. Three very large leaves attach to a main stem. They branch pinnately 2 to 4 times and bear many oval or lance-shaped leaflets that sometimes coalesce at the base. The delicate, light green leaflets, 1 to 2 1/2 inches long, wear a bluish, glaucous coating. One or more tight racemes of showy flowers terminate stem ends. The flowers, composed of 4 petals in 2 pairs, attach to short pedicels in the middle. An upper petal about 1 inch long forms both an upper hood and a long tapering spur, while the lower petal creates an open mouth. Both of these outermost petals have pretty crests parallel to the axis of the flower. These unusual blooms point in all directions around the stem and change from white or pale pink to deep rose or purple on each blossom. April to July for this one. HABITAT: Moist shady woods from low to quite high elevations. RANGE: Southern British Columbia to NW Oregon, from the W Cascades to the coast.

WILD BLEEDING HEART

Dicentra formosa. Heart-shaped describes the flowers of this choice plant. The 3/4-inch blooms hang in branched clusters—a panicle. Pink to rose shades favor these memorable blossoms. The plants spread from rhizomes and may form quite large patches, the stems and leaves sometimes rising nearly 2 feet. Similar to the leaves of Dutchman's breeches, the leaflet lobes spread somewhat wider. The delicately fragrant flowers open from March to July depending on elevation and moisture availability. HABITAT: Moist woods or fairly dry, open areas; low to mid-montane altitudes. RANGE: Southern British Columbia to central California in the Cascade and Coast ranges.

Bleeding Heart Family *(Fumariaceae)*

DUTCHMAN'S BREECHES

Dicentra cucullaria. Appearing quite similar to the unmistakable bleeding hearts, Dutchman's breeches sends up one or more unbranched floral stems, 6 to 18 inches high, that end in three- to eight-flowered, pendent racemes. Each blossom displays two petals and mostly hides two. The outer two have spurs at the base about 1/2 inch long that resemble baggy pant legs hanging upside down, from which comes the common name. The white or pale pink flowers also flare at the end and display yellow tips. One or more compound leaves sprout directly from the root and grow nearly as high as the flowers. Long leaf petioles branch pinnately two or three times and the many leaflets also divide into narrow lobes. The overall effect is almost fernlike, and a bluish glaucous coat covers the succulent leaves. It blooms in spring. HABITAT: Moist woods and gravelly stream banks. RANGE: Generally along the Columbia River, W Oregon and Washington to tributaries in the Blue Mountains of E Oregon, Washington and adjacent Idaho.

Gentian Family *(Gentianaceae)*

Gentian Family *(Gentianaceae)*

COLUMBIA FRASERA, COLUMBO
Frasera albicaulis. A tuft of smooth,
narrow leaves grows 4 to 28 inches tall,
the leaf margins prominently outlined in
white. Three veins mark the leaves that
grow widest near the end (spatula
shaped). Shorter stem leaves attach in a
few opposite pairs to one or more
unbranched floral stems. One to several
tight clusters of flowers adorn the
stems. The open-faced (rotate) flowers
display four lance-shaped petals that
range from white to pale or rather dark
blue, generally mottled with darker
shades of blue or purple. Each petal
face bears a rather long or linear gland
that is lined with decorative hairs. Five
varieties of Columbia frasera bloom
from May into July. HABITAT:
Bunchgrass or sagebrush plains into the
foothills and open woods. RANGE: East
slope of the Cascades, S British
Columbia to SW Montana and the Great
Basin to NW California. COMMENT: The
attractive white blooms of white-
stemmed frasera appear very similar to
this species. It is endemic to the
mountains of South-central Idaho.

MONUMENT PLANT, GREEN GENTIAN
Frasera speciosa. A tuft or rosette of
leaves, smooth and oblong or lance-
shaped, to 20 inches long, grows for
perhaps 20 to 60 years without
blooming. Finally one central,
unbranched stem, 2 to 5 feet tall,
shoots up, bearing many whorls of
stem leaves that reduce upwards. After
blooming once these stately, conical
plants then die. Numerous flowers erupt
from the axils of the upper leaf whorls.
From a distance the flowers appear
quite plain, but on close inspection they
are stunning. Purple flecks dot the four
greenish white, open-faced petals.
Pinkish hairs fringe two oval or linear
nectary glands near the base of each
petal. Four gracefully curving stamens
and a deeply divided, hair-like corona
surround a prominent green ovary at
the center of the blossom in June and
July. The dried stalks may remain
standing for several years. HABITAT:
High prairies to subalpine and alpine
slopes and meadows. RANGE: Eastern
Washington to the Black Hills and south
into Mexico.

Gentian Family *(Gentianaceae)*

Gentian Family *(Gentianaceae)*

EXPLORER'S GENTIAN, BOG GENTIAN

Gentiana calycosa. Dark blue to purple (rarely yellowish) bells, about 1 1/2 inches long, stand upright and open to the sun. Greenish yellow speckles mottle the bells inside, and they typically fade to green or pale yellow at the base. The flowers display five rounded petal lobes with pleats between the lobes. Each pleat usually ends in two fine, sharp-pointed teeth between the petals. Several stems, 2 to 10 inches tall, grow in a tuft from a fleshy root. Solitary flowers, or occasionally as many as three, terminate the stems. Smooth opposite leaves attach sessile on stems and a pair of basal leaves fuse together encircling the stem. These elegant blooms open in summer. HABITAT: Moist alpine or subalpine sites on fairly deep soil. RANGE: Widespread in the high mountains of North America.

STAFF GENTIAN

Gentiana sceptrum. The upright blue cups of another gentian perch atop the stems of a tufted perennial, 8 to 20 inches or taller. Several flowers with five petals may show dark greenish spots both inside and out. Sometimes the blooms seem to open with considerable reluctance. Plaits between the petal lobes do not exhibit the toothed appendages of explorer's gentian. Lance shaped leaves clasp the stem in opposite pairs, growing smaller down the stem, reduced to sheathing bracts at the base. The flowers appear in mid to late summer. HABITAT: Lake and stream banks, bogs and wet meadows and moist sandy flats behind coastal dunes. RANGE: British Columbia to NW California, west of the Cascades, most commonly along the coast.

Geranium Family (*Geraniaceae*)

Gooseberry Family (*Grossulariaceae*)

RICHARDSON'S GERANIUM or CRANESBILL

Geranium richardsonii. Five white or pale pink petals, beautifully lined with purple stripes distinguish this choice geranium. The flowers spread about 1 to 1 1/2 inches across, usually in sparsely branched clusters (cymes). The plants grow 1 to 2 1/2 feet high in spreading clumps. Most of the leaves sprout directly from the root on long petioles, but a few smaller leaves attach at stem nodes. The larger leaves spread five or seven palmate lobes, 3 to 5 inches broad. The lobes are cleft about 3/4 of the leaf length, and a few sharp teeth serrate the edges. It blooms in summer. HABITAT: Prefers some forest shade from low to subalpine elevations. RANGE: Southeastern British Columbia to Saskatchewan and south to S California and New Mexico, east of the Cascade-Sierras. COMMENT: Richardson's and sticky geranium sometimes hybridize, producing pretty pink flowers.

LOBB'S GOOSEBERRY

Ribes lobbii. As a rule of thumb, gooseberry bushes bear thorns and currants go unarmed. This branching, spreading shrub reaches 4 feet high, and three sharp spines arm each node. Distinctive flowers, one or two hanging pendent from each node, feature five sepals joined in a tube for half their length, and then rounded lobes flare backward. These expose gorgeous, dark maroon to brownish faces. Then five white or pink petals protrude in a contrasting cylinder and five delicate stamens, tipped with reddish anthers, complete the stunning array. One inch leaves have three to five lobes and margins with irregular rounded teeth. The leaves erupt from the nodes and wear sticky glands on both surfaces. The round, hairy berries, greenish or reddish, are not palatable. Blooms generally appear in April and May. HABITAT: Partial shade to openings, valleys to montane. RANGE: British Columbia to NW California from the Cascades to the coast. COMMENT: This makes a fine ornamental. If starting with native plants, take a few cuttings in spring or fall, but do not try to transplant an entire bush.

Geranium Family *(Geraniaceae)*

STICKY GERANIUM, CRANESBILL

Geranium viscosissimum. Resplendent, open-faced flowers about 2 inches across, which vary in color from pink to fuschia and occasionally white, grace this leafy, branching perennial, 1 1/2 to 3 feet tall. Dark red or purple veins line the petals, while five to seven lobes divide the leaves nearly to the base. The lobes possess sharp, irregular teeth. In fruit the petals fall off, but the pointed stigma and style elongate to about 1 inch and resemble a crane's bill. Sticky geranium blooms commonly from May to August. HABITAT: Open prairies to scattered forests from low to rather high elevations. RANGE: British Columbia to Saskatchewan and south to California and Colorado. COMMENT: Seven species of *Geranium* grow wild in our area, three of them introduced from Europe.

Gooseberry Family (*Grossulariaceae*)

Gooseberry Family (*Grossulariaceae*)

ALPINE PRICKLY CURRANT, MOUNTAIN GOOSEBERRY

Ribes montigenum. Alpine prickly
currant only grows 10 to 20 inches high,
its stems branched and sprawling. It
produces a few slender spines at stem
nodes. Few-flowered racemes of small,
greenish-yellow or pinkish, saucer-
shaped blossoms originate in leaf axils.
The leaf blades spread about 1 inch
wide with five deeply cut lobes and
irregular teeth on the margins. Rather
bristly hairs generously coat the leaves.
Small, reddish, edible berries develop in
the autumn. It's an early summer
bloomer. HABITAT: Alpine and subalpine
on rocky terrain. RANGE: East slope of
Cascades and Sierras to the Rockies.
COMMENT: Swamp gooseberry, *R.
lacustre*, produces similar appearing
flowers, but lacks the gland-tipped hairs
on leaf blades.

STICKY CURRANT

Ribes viscosissimum. Sticky currant is
well named with viscid, gland-tipped
hairs on twigs, foliage, flowers and fruit.
A rather unpleasant odor also attends
the plant. The branching, spreading
shrub normally grows less than 6 feet
high and has no spines. Clustered
racemes of six to twelve flowers
terminate twig ends. The calyx forms a
tube with spreading lobes that may
show green, yellowish or red-purple
coloration. Five short, rounded petals
continue the tube. Nearly black, oval
berries are dry and bitter. Leaves have
three or five lobes and rounded scallops
on the edges. The flowers open in May
and June. HABITAT: A forest understory
species on both wet and dry sites.
RANGE: British Columbia to California
from the east slope Cascades and
Sierras to Alberta and Arizona.

Gooseberry Family *(Grossulariaceae)*

RED FLOWERED CURRANT

Ribes sanguineum. A raceme of 10 to 20 small flowers with red to crimson sepals and white to red petals highlight this shrub. The calyx forms a cylinder, from the lip of which five round lobes open wide. Several woody stems spread into a loose bush, generally 3 to 9 feet tall. Leaves have three or five lobes, the blades quite crinkled, and the margins reveal many small teeth. Blue or purple berries, insipid if not unpalatable, develop in summer or fall. Look for these striking blooms in spring. HABITAT: Shady woods to dry, open or rocky sites. RANGE: Cascades to the coast, S British Columbia to central California. COMMENT: It makes a choice ornamental shrub.

SYRINGA, MOCK ORANGE

Philadelphous lewisii. This shrub, the state flower of Idaho, reaches 3 to 9 feet high and displays showy white, four-petaled flowers that cluster on side branches. They emit a very sweet fragrance remindful of orange blossoms. The elliptic or lance-shaped leaves generally reach 1 to 3 inches long. Native Americans used the straight young shoots for making arrows. It blooms from May to July. HABITAT: Dry rocky hillsides or talus slopes or along stream beds to open or scattered forests. RANGE: West of the continental divide in Montana to the Pacific Coast from British Columbia to California.

Hydrangea Family *(Hydrangeaceae)*

Waterleaf Family *(Hydrophyllaceae)*

DWARF HESPEROCHIRON

Hesperochiron pumilus. These gay little beauties hug the ground among a rosette of narrow elliptical leaves. They exhibit purple anthers, while prominent blue or purple veins draw a lacy pattern on two or more white, saucer-shaped flowers on each plant. A short leafless stem sprouts directly from the root crown to support each flower. Look for them soon after snow melt. HABITAT: Forest openings, scattered timber and meadows from foothills to rather high montane elevations. RANGE: Western United States east of the Cascades. COMMENT: A somewhat larger species, *H. californicus,* bears more than five flowers.

149

Waterleaf Family *(Hydrophyllaceae)*

BALLHEAD WATERLEAF

Hydrophyllum capitatum. These stunning floral balls, ordinarily blue but occasionally white, have many protruding stamens that make them look like pincushions. Coarse teeth serrate the margins of a few relatively large and deeply lobed leaves. They bloom early in the season. HABITAT: River bottoms, prairies and open woods from low to moderate elevations. RANGE: East of the Cascade summit from S Canada to Montana, Colorado and California. COMMENT: On two varieties the flowers attach below the leaves. A third variety frequents the Columbia Gorge and holds its flowers well above the leaves.

Waterleaf Family *(Hydrophyllaceae)*

PACIFIC (SLENDER) WATERLEAF

Hydrophyllum tenuipes. This perennial waterleaf sends up a single stem 1 to 2 feet or more. Three large leaves attach alternately along the stem. The leaves are both palmately and pinnately compound. All leaflets display coarse, sharp-pointed, irregular teeth. The cup-shaped blossoms form a rather open inflorescence. White to greenish flowers are common, but blue or purple blooms do occur locally. Like other waterleafs, the stamens project well out of the floral cups, blooming from May to July. HABITAT: Moist woods at lower levels. RANGE: Western foothills of the Cascades to the coast, SW British Columbia to N California.

Waterleaf Family *(Hydrophyllaceae)*

BABY BLUE EYES

Nemophila menziesii var. *atomaria.* The exquisite flowers of this little annual consist of five rounded petals that open from a short floral tube. Upon a stark white base, several rows of stylish, purple-black spots radiate outward in a lustrous display. Slender pedicels support the blossoms. The deeply lobed, pinnate leaves attach mostly opposite on the stems. Several stems sprawl or rise 2 to 12 inches high on each plant. These unique flowers bloom mostly in April. HABITAT: Moist sites, open or shaded. RANGE: Low elevations of W Oregon to Baja. COMMENT: The common name, baby blue eyes, comes from blue-flowered varieties that inhabit California.

Waterleaf Family *(Hydrophyllaceae)* **Waterleaf Family** *(Hydrophyllaceae)*

WHITELEAF PHACELIA

Phacelia hastata. Whiteleaf or silverleaf phacelia takes its name from the coating of silvery hairs on elliptical or lance-shaped leaves that grow mostly in a basal tuft. Prominent veins, nearly parallel, mark the leaf blades. Several stems, 8 to 24 inches long, spread at the base before turning upright or lie prostrate on the ground. Numerous helical coils of small flowers bear stiff bristly hairs on the calyces. The compact blooms are white to pale lavender (on the alpine variety shown), small and bell-shaped with protruding stamens. Flowers open ordinarily in June and July. HABITAT: Dry, sandy or rocky sites from prairies to scattered timber to alpine. RANGE: Southwestern Canada to California and Nebraska. COMMENT: Whiteleaf phacelia has five varieties that vary from tall, erect plants to low, prostrate ones. Furthermore, varileaf phacelia, *P. heterophylla,* is very similar, but has two lateral lobes on the leaves.

THREADLEAF PHACELIA

Phacelia linearis. This slender annual may send up one simple stem, 5 to 20 inches high, or branch rather profusely. Narrow, simple leaves grow on the stem, or the leaves may develop two lateral lobes near the base of the plant. Several delicate flowers, 1/2 to 3/4 inch across, crowd the stem tips. They are quite the largest blossoms of all our native phacelias. From a short tube flare five rounded petals in a saucer shape, pale blue, lavender or pinkish. Threadleaf phacelia blooms in spring. HABITAT: Grassy fields, dry prairies and foothills to medium elevation. RANGE: Southern British Columbia and Alberta to N California and Wyoming.

Waterleaf Family *(Hydrophyllaceae)*

St. Johnswort Family *(Hypericaceae)*

SILKY PHACELIA, PURPLE FRINGE

Phacelia sericea. A dense column of tiny purple flowers clothes the upper 1/4 to 1/3 of one or more stems that rise in a clump 6 to 16 inches high. Close inspection will reveal that the flowers actually grow in very small, helical coils. Many hair-like stamens, tipped with minute yellow anthers, project well out of the flowers. Most of the leaves attach basally on long petioles. Densely coated with silvery hairs, the pinnately dissected or toothed leaves provide a lustrous background for these common and easily recognized flowers. They bloom from late spring into summer. HABITAT: Rocky or gravelly meadows and dry slopes in subalpine and alpine terrain. RANGE: Southwestern Canada to N California and New Mexico. COMMENT: We have more than 20 species of *Phacelia* in the Northwest.

WESTERN ST. JOHNSWORT

Hypericum formosum. Joyous yellow flowers spread five petals about 1/2 inch across. Tiny black dots may line the margins of the petals. Many yellow stamens explode in a starburst around a prominent, superior ovary that ages from green to yellow to bright red. Flower buds, commonly tinged with red, also provide a delightful contrast to the opened blooms. The low-spreading perennial sends up many slender stems to 8 inches tall. Shiny green leaves attach in opposite pairs and the flowers sprout from the axils of the uppermost leaves throughout the summer. HABITAT: Wet or moist sites from the seacoast to high alpine. RANGE: Southwestern Canada into Mexico, mostly in the high mountains.

153

Mint Family *(Lamiaceae)*

WILD BERGAMOT, BEE BALM

Monarda fistulosa. Wild bergamot develops an upright, terminal head of pink or purplish flowers. Each blossom, 1 to 1 1/2 inches long, has two lips consisting of a narrow hood above and a spreading, three-lobed lip. Two stamens protrude from the hood. The simple stems, coated with fine hairs, stand 1 to 2 feet tall. Lance-shaped and toothed leaves all attach to the stems in pairs. It blooms in early summer. HABITAT: Open meadows and slopes from valleys to subalpine. RANGE: Southern British Columbia to Montana, Quebec, Georgia and Mexico, mostly in the Rockies eastward. COMMENT: Mountain monardella, *Monardella odoratissima*, is a smaller plant that normally grows in tight clumps.

Mint Family *(Lamiaceae)*

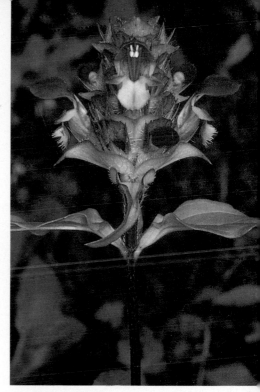

Mint Family *(Lamiaceae)*

FIELD MINT

Mentha arvensis. Square stems rise 1 to 3 feet from a spreading, underground rhizome. At regular nodes along the stem, lance-shaped, opposite leaves attach on very short petioles and project horizontally. Many sharp teeth serrate the leaf edges. Tight clusters of small, 1/4-inch, cup-shaped flowers nestle in the axils of the upper and middle leaves. These white, or more commonly lavender or pink, blossoms extend numerous stamens. When crushed, the leaves and stems emit a strong minty fragrance. The flowers appear in mid to late summer. HABITAT: Damp ground, especially stream banks. RANGE: Throughout much of the N hemisphere. COMMENT: One can brew a pleasing cup of tea from the leaves and stems.

SELFHEAL, HEALALL

Prunella vulgaris. Several dainty purple flowers adorn a short, thick spike of alternating flowers and dark bracts. A rounded upper lip forms a graceful hood above the lower, which has three lobes. A pretty fringe graces the central lobe. These plants usually stand 4 to 8 inches tall and bear a few oval leaves. Blooms early to late in the season. HABITAT: Moist ground, both open and wooded. RANGE: Widespread throughout much of the world. COMMENT: The boiled leaves make a refreshing, minty tea, said to have medicinal qualities.

Mint Family *(Lamiaceae)*

Mint Family *(Lamiaceae)*

NARROWLEAVED SKULLCAP

Scutellaria angustifolia. These navy blue to violet flowers attach in the axils of opposite leaves and converge outward, side by side from the stem in pairs. The tubular, upcurving corolla, about 1 inch long, spreads four petal lobes—a broad hairy lower lip, an upper hood and two small lobes on·the sides. The two-lipped calyx develops a peculiar, raised crest on top that distinguishes skullcaps. The 4 to 12 inch tall stems normally branch near the base and rise from perennial rhizomes. Smooth, narrowly oval or lance-shaped leaves reach about 1 inch or less. Blooms appear from mid spring to early summer. HABITAT: Dry, rocky canyons, plains and foothills into the lower mountains. RANGE: East of the Cascades from S British Columbia to Idaho and California. Occasional in the Willamette Valley. COMMENT: Botanists recognize five closely related species of *Scutellaria* in our region.

PURPLE SAGE, GRAYBALL SAGE

Salvia dorrii.

Mint Family *(Lamiaceae)*

PURPLE SAGE, GRAYBALL SAGE

Salvia dorrii. Made famous by a Zane Grey novel, these low, rounded bushes often grow wider than high (2 feet high or less) and carry silvery, hairy leaves that spread widest near the tip. In full bloom clusters of breathtaking flowers literally cover these shrubs. The blooms vary from occasional white to deep purple. The 1/2 inch long blossoms open broad, drooping lower lips with ragged fringes on the margins, two lateral petals each and two-lobed upper lips. Two stamens and one style project out of each tube. Many rounded, hairy bracts, 1/4 to 1/2 inch long and usually reddish or coppery tinted, provide a conspicuous setting for the flowers. May and June for this one. HABITAT: Dry plains and slopes, often rocky or sandy with sagebrush. RANGE: Central Washington to S Idaho, Arizona and S California. COMMENT: Three rather weedy, alien species of *Salvia*, not to be confused with sagebrush, also occur in the Northwest.

Mint Family *(Lamiaceae)*

Mint Family *(Lamiaceae)*

GREAT HEDGE NETTLE

Stachys cooleyae. Standing 2 to 5 feet tall among lush forest vegetation, this largest of the hedge nettles displays a spike of splashy magenta flowers, blooming from the bottom upward. Each floral tube opens a drooping, three-lobed lower lip, 1/3 to 1/2 inch long and a shorter upper hood. Four stamens and a single style reveal themselves in the throat of the tube. The flowers sprout in whorls of three or more in the axils of upper leaves and bracts. The oval, roundly toothed leaves attach in opposite pairs on the stem. Stems, leaves, bracts and calyces all bear coats of stiff, more or less sticky, gland-tipped hairs. The plants often occur in patches, growing from stout underground rhizomes. One may find the blooms from June into August. HABITAT: Streambanks and other wet ground. RANGE: Cascades to the Coast, S British Columbia to S Oregon. COMMENT: This is one of four species of hedge nettle in the Northwest.

MEXICAN BETONY

Stachys mexicana. Mexican betony is a smaller version of great hedge nettle. Its stems reach 12 to 32 inches tall. The flowers grow in whorls or interrupted spikes on the upper stem. Floral tubes are 1/3 to 1/2 inch long and purple and white spots mottle the pink or reddish blossoms. Oval or lance-shaped leaves grow 2 to 5 inches long, toothed on the margins and quite hairy. Look for the flowers in early summer. HABITAT: Wet places or bogs in forested areas. RANGE: British Columbia to California, mainly in the Coast Range, but occasional in the Willamette Valley.

Bladderwort Family *(Lentibulariaceae)*   **Flax Family** *(Linaceae)*

COMMON BUTTERWORT

Pinguicula vulgaris. These lovely, solitary, blue-violet flowers on slender unbranched stems, 2 to 5 inches tall, resemble violets at first glance. Of the five unequal petal lobes, the lower one projects outward the farthest. The floral tube extends backward into a narrow cone or spur. Two-inch long leaves form a basal rosette. Sticky glands cover these pale green or yellowish leaves causing small insects to stick to them. Enzymes in the sticky exudate digest the insects and extract their juices, leaving only insect skeletons behind. Because the water in high mountains, especially near snow banks, lacks minerals and nutrients, the plant uses insects to supplement its nutrient needs. Look for this fascinating little carnivore in midsummer. HABITAT: Wet mossy seeps and bogs from high montane to alpine. RANGE: Circumpolar, south to Montana and N California. Rare throughout much of its range.

WILD BLUE FLAX

Linum perenne var. *lewisii.* Several slender stems originate from the top of a woody perennial root. The bright blue, five-petaled, open-faced flowers, 1 to 2 inches in diameter, perch atop the stems. Only a few blossoms open at one time. Leaves are short, linear, upright and closely spaced on the stem. Blooms from May to July. HABITAT: Dry prairie and grassy foothills to subalpine slopes. RANGE: Most of North America west of the Mississippi River as well as Europe and Asia. COMMENT: Our native variety of wild blue flax can only be distinguished from two Old World varieties on technical characteristics. In times past one of the latter was introduced and cultivated extensively for the production of linen fiber and linseed oil. Synthetic products have replaced flax for these uses today.

Blazing Star Family *(Loasaceae)*

BLAZING STAR

Mentzelia laevicaulis. This coarse, many-branched perennial or biennial, 1 to 3 feet tall, bears large, handsome flowers, 2 to 4 inches across. The lemon yellow blossoms have five lance-shaped petals that spread widely around a multitude of stamens. Blazing star opens at night and closes during the heat of the day. The large leaves have serrate edges and barbed hairs that scratch or grab onto clothing. Look for blazing star to bloom in mid to late summer. HABITAT: Dry desert or steep south facing slopes. RANGE: Central British Columbia to Montana, Colorado and California. COMMENT: Another species of blazing star, *M. decapetala*, has 10 petals instead of 5.

Mallow Family *(Malvaceae)*

Mallow Family *(Malvaceae)*

OREGON CHECKERMALLOW
Sidalcea oregana. The plants and flowers of Oregon checkermallow vary considerably through two subspecies and five varieties. Five lovely petals in various shades of pink have rounded notches at the tip. The unbranched stems stand 8 to 60 inches tall and feel rough to the touch, because of many stiff, star-clustered hairs. The palmately veined leaf shape depends upon the variety, from shallowly lobed to deeply divided. Look for them from late spring to mid summer. HABITAT: Meadows and woods at low to medium elevation. RANGE: Central Washington to W Montana, N California, Utah and Wyoming.

MUNRO'S GLOBEMALLOW, WHITE LEAVED GLOBEMALLOW
Sphaeralcea munroana. Numerous brick red or reddish-orange flowers bloom along the upper stem in a narrow, open raceme. Several of these unbranching stems, 1 1/2 to 2 1/2 feet long, sprawl in a clump from a strong perennial taproot. The grayish, hairy leaves spread palmately and somewhat delta-shaped and wear coats of soft downy hairs. Three or five very shallow leaf lobes distinguish this species, and small rounded scallops on the edges complete the adornment. It bursts into bloom from May into summer. HABITAT: Dry sagebrush prairies and mountain foothills. RANGE: Southern British Columbia, east of the Cascades, to W Montana, California and Utah.

Mallow Family *(Malvaceae)*

GLOBE MALLOW, WILD HOLLYHOCK

Iliamna rivularis. These gorgeous pink hollyhocks open 2 to 3 inches wide on stout unbranching stems, normally 3 to 5 feet tall. A spike-like raceme describes the floral arrangement. The large maple-shaped leaves spread three to seven lobes. The flowers bloom in summer. HABITAT: Rivularis means stream bank, a common habitat. Also found in other moist places in the mountains, especially on disturbed or burned over areas. RANGE: Southeastern British Columbia and SW Alberta to Oregon, east of the Cascade summit, and Colorado. COMMENT: The seeds of globe mallow usually require some scouring, such as running water or heat from a fire, before they will germinate.

Mallow Family *(Malvaceae)*

CHECKERBLOOM

Sidalcea malvaeflora subspecies *asprella* var. *virgata*. Checkerbloom raises hairy stems 1 to 2 feet long that ordinarily lean and curve near the bottom. Numerous blossoms 1/2 to 1 1/4 inches across form spectacular open racemes. Two kinds of flowers may develop— larger perfect flowers with both stamens and pistils and smaller blooms with only fertile pistils. They may vary from pale pink to magenta. The leaves are nearly round in outline. Near the base palmate veins end in shallow scallops, while upper leaves are deeply cleft into narrow lobes. They bloom in springtime. HABITAT: Moist meadows, roadsides and open hills at lower elevations. RANGE: Southwestern Oregon from the upper Willamette Valley through much of California.

Water Lily Family *(Nymphaeaceae)*

YELLOW WATER LILY

Nuphar polysepalum. This aquatic herb grows from a thick rhizome buried in mud under standing water. Thick round stems, up to 6 feet long, rise to the surface and anchor floating leaves or flowers. The roundly heart-shaped, leathery leaves are 4 to 16 inches across. Brilliant yellow or reddish-tinged, cup-shaped blossoms reach 3 or 4 inches wide. A squat, yellow, toadstool-shaped stigma occupies the center of the blossom. Late spring through summer. HABITAT: Shallow ponds, lake edges or slow-moving streams. RANGE: Alaska to Alberta, N California and Colorado. COMMENT: We have two native yellow species and two white ones that come from E North America.

Evening Primrose Family *(Onagraceae)*

FAREWELL TO SPRING, HERALD OF SUMMER

Clarkia amoena. As the heat of summer dries up the grasses and early wildflowers, farewell to spring begins to bloom. Quite variable in size through three varieties, the annual plants may raise a single, 3-inch stem on poor sites, but branch and sprawl 3 feet on deeper soil. The flowers open four rounded petals, about 1 inch long in a cup or saucer shape, that may vary from pale pink to dark magenta. Darker crimson to purple often splashes the center of each petal. Beneath the flower four reddish sepals cohere and turn to one side. Narrow, entire leaves, 1 to 3 inches long, alternate on the stems. Blooming happens from June into August. HABITAT: Dry grassy fields and hills to forest openings. RANGE: The coast to the W Cascades, S British Columbia to central California. COMMENT: The stems supporting flower buds of this species stand mostly erect, in contrast to slender godetia, *C. gracilis*, which nods its inflorescence until the blossoms open.

Evening Primrose Family *(Onagraceae)*

Evening Primrose Family *(Onagraceae)*

BEACH EVENING PRIMROSE

Camissonia cheiranthifolia. From a perennial root system deeply buried in sand spreads a pleasing rosette of lance shaped basal leaves, 2 to 3 inches long, that are broadest near the end. Several reddish-tinted, prostrate branches radiate outward from the rosette, up to 24 inches. Smaller leaves grow irregularly on the stems. Bright yellow, four-petaled flowers, about 1/2 inch across, attach sessile in the axils of leaves near the stem ends from April into August. The blossoms often turn red with age. HABITAT: Beaches, dunes and sand flats along the coast. RANGE: Oregon to Baja.

CLARKIA, RAGGED ROBIN

Clarkia pulchella. These unique blossoms have four pink or rose and deeply three-lobed petals, a four-lobed pearly white stigma and four tightly coiled anthers. Clarkia is an annual herb, 4 to 20 inches long, that frequently droops and is supported by grass. It blooms in May and June, sometimes turning entire hillsides bright pink. HABITAT: Loves open grassy hillsides. RANGE: South-central British Columbia to E Oregon and W Montana. COMMENT: Capt. William Clark, of Lewis and Clark fame, lends his name to this genus. Native only to W America, *Clarkia* includes about 30 species. The others bear little resemblance to this one, however.

Evening Primrose Family *(Onagraceae)* · **Evening Primrose Family** *(Onagraceae)*

COMMON CLARKIA

Clarkia rhomboidea. Four pink to deep rose petals, arranged irregularly, often reveal dark purple spots on close scrutiny. The four-sided petals, 1/4 to 1/2 inch long, are slightly rhomboid in shape and supported by a narrow stalk called a claw that normally has a couple of little teeth on the edges. The annual stem rises 6 to 40 inches tall and carries its flowers in an open raceme, blooming only a few at a time. The unopened buds tend to nod. A few lance-shaped leaves 1/2 to 1 1/4 inches long scatter in opposite pairs on the stems. Look for these little beauties in early summer. HABITAT: Dry grassy places into forests of lower foothills and mountains. RANGE: Southern British Columbia east of the Cascades, to the edge of W Montana and south to Arizona and S California.

FIREWEED

Epilobium angustifolium. Tall spires of pink to purple flowers often grow in masses from aggressive rhizomes. The flowers have four rounded petals, wide-spreading and arranged somewhat irregularly. They bloom from the bottom upward, several at a time, so that a stem often has seed pods below, flowers and unopened buds above. In autumn the seed pods burst and release masses of tiny seeds held in cottony hairs that disperse readily on the wind. The stems, mostly unbranched, rise 3 to 10 feet tall. Alternate, lance-shaped leaves grow 4 to 6 inches long and nearly sessile. Blooming occurs throughout the summer. HABITAT: From low elevation to high in the mountains. RANGE: Much of the N hemisphere. COMMENT: Fireweed commonly invades burned over land and clearcut forest areas. It is a valuable pioneer species on denuded land and tends to die out when forests regenerate.

166

Evening Primrose Family *(Onagraceae)*

RED WILLOWHERB, ALPINE FIREWEED

Epilobium latifolium. Gorgeous four-petaled, magenta or occasionally albino flowers welcome the alpine explorer. Three to twelve flowers originate in the axils of the uppermost leaves and form a raceme on reddish branch ends. The plants, either upright or reclining, produce 4- to 16-inch stems. A fine blue, glaucous coating tints the oval leaves. They bloom through the summer. HABITAT: Scree slopes, gravel bars and stream banks, alpine and subalpine. RANGE: Arctic regions and high mountains, south to Colorado and the Sierras.

Evening Primrose Family *(Onagraceae)*

HOOKER'S EVENING PRIMROSE

Oenothera hookeri (O. elata). Spectacular yellow flowers, 2 to 3 inches across, grace simple or few-branched stems, 1 1/2 to 3 feet tall. The inflorescence forms a spike, but the base of the flower tapers to a slender tube about 1 1/2 inches long that looks like a stem. The flowers bloom one or a few at a time, opening in the evening or at night. They usually wilt in the heat of the day, turning reddish, and drop off early. New buds are then ready to open by the next evening. Leaves are narrow and alternate on the stem. This beauty blooms from summer into early fall. HABITAT: Variable from open prairie to the lower mountains. RANGE: Eastern Washington to Texas and Baja. COMMENT: Common evening primrose, *O. strigosa,* appears quite similar to this species, but the plants are smaller and flowers reach less than 2 inches across.

WHITE-STEMMED EVENING PRIMROSE

Oenothera pallida. Whitish, peeling bark on branching, semiwoody stems to 20 inches tall identifies this species. Numerous fragrant, white flowers, about 2 inches across, attach to the stems in leafy spikes. From pink buds the blossoms open in the evening and turn pink in the heat of the next day. Night flying insects pollinate the flowers. Many narrow, linear leaves, usually toothed on the edges, sometimes display basal lobes. The flowers open mostly in June and July. HABITAT: Sand dunes or gravelly slopes, often with sagebrush. RANGE: Central Washington to Montana and Nebraska, south on both sides of the Rockies to Mexico.

Evening Primrose Family *(Onagraceae)*

Evening Primrose Family *(Onagraceae)*

TANSYLEAF EVENING PRIMROSE

Camissonia tanacetifolia (Oenothera tanacetifolia). Several bright yellow, four-petaled blossoms, about 1 inch in diameter, perch 1 to 3 1/2 inches above a rosette of deeply lobed or cut leaves. A stalk supporting each flower is actually a slender tube and part of the blossom. It connects the ovary, attached to the top of the taproot, to the showy part of the flower. The petals often turn purple with age. Blooming occurs from May into summer. HABITAT: Sagebrush plains to pine woods, often on disturbed ground. RANGE: Columbia and Great Basins. COMMENT: We have no less than four species of low, yellow evening primroses in the Northwest.

Broomrape Family *(Orobanchaceae)*

Broomrape Family *(Orobanchaceae)*

GROUND CONE

Boschniakia strobilacea. This plant is often overlooked, because it resembles a pine cone lying on the forest floor. The fleshy root of this parasite attaches to the roots of a host plant, often salal. Above ground, tightly overlapping leaf scales cover a succulent, hairless stem, 1 1/2 to 2 inches in diameter and 4 to 10 inches high. Reddish-brown or yellowish coloration helps camouflage the beguiling ground cone. From May to July small, two-lipped flowers form a dense spike in the axils of the upper scales. HABITAT: Forest duff. RANGE: Coastal mountains, SW Oregon to California. COMMENT: Pogue, *B. hookeri,* a similar but smaller species, resides near the coast from Alaska to California.

CLOVER BROOMRAPE

Orobanche minor. This alien parasite usually attaches to the roots of members of the pea or sunflower families, and especially thrives with clover as its host. Unbranched stems may reach 20 inches in height. Numerous 1/2-inch flowers rest on the stem without pedicels, making a floral spike. The tubular corollas are usually white or yellow with delicate lilac hues tinting the outside near the end. Ragged little scallops mark the ends of the petal lobes. The calyx splits top and bottom, and the lateral sections have two sharp-pointed lobes of different length. A single, lance-shaped bract, brownish-purple to match the calyx, subtends each flower. HABITAT: Low elevation fields and woods. RANGE: Native of Europe and introduced in many parts of the world—W Oregon and Washington in our area.

Broomrape Family *(Orobanchaceae)*

FLAT TOPPED BROOMRAPE, CLUSTERED CANCERROOT

Orobanche corymbosa. This root parasite produces a cluster of somewhat curved, tube-shaped flowers that open at or slightly above ground line. A succulent stem, 1/2 to 1 inch thick and about 4 inches long, is buried under ground and branches in a corymb, making an inflorescence generally flat on top. The flowers, 1 inch long or less, open two lips: the upper with two rounded lobes and the lower with three acute lobes. Color varies from white to yellow to purple or brown, lined with purple stripes, and the upper petals usually show some purple, especially on the inner surface. Four or five calyx lobes also nearly reach the length of the flower tube. Four anthers inside the tube wear heavy woolly beards. They bloom in summer. HABITAT: Dry plains and canyons. RANGE: Southern British Columbia, south through the Columbia and Great Basins. COMMENT: This species can easily be confused with the closely related California broomrape, *O. californica.*

Broomrape Family *(Orobanchaceae)*

Wood Sorrel Family *(Oxalidaceae)*

ONE FLOWERED CANCERROOT, NAKED BROOMRAPE

Orobanche uniflora. This wee root parasite usually does not exceed 4 inches in height. It feeds on the roots of many other species. Most commonly each plant sends up only one unbranched stem, but occasionally two or three branches will occur. A single tubular, two-lipped flower, 3/4 to 1 1/4 inches long, crowns each stem. Dark purple stripes often beautify the blossom and two ridges on the lower lip carry pretty yellow tints. Pale yellow to lilac or purple, the flowers assume a noticeable downward bend in the middle. Sticky, glandular hairs liberally coat the stems and flowers. The plants have no functional leaves and only a few alternate scales appear on the stems. Blooms can occur from early spring to midsummer. HABITAT: Open areas, preferring mossy rock outcrops, sagebrush prairies into the mountains. RANGE: Most of North America, north of Mexico.

REDWOOD SORREL

Oxalis oregana. Making a luxuriant ground cover on the forest floor, redwood sorrel sends up both leaf and floral stems from scaly rhizomatous root nodes. Hairy leaf stems, 2 to 8 inches tall, each support three broad, heart-shaped leaflets, notched at the tip, that resemble clover or shamrock leaves. The flower stalks are shorter than the leaves, 2 to 6 inches, and carry solitary five-petaled, funnel-shaped flowers. White or pink with lovely red or purple veins, the petals reach 1/2 to 3/4 inch in length. Blooming mostly in April and May, the blossoms often refuse to open in wet, cloudy weather. HABITAT: Deep shady woods. RANGE: Both sides of the Cascades to the coast, Washington to central California. COMMENT: Redwood sorrel transplants easily to the flower garden, but can become an invasive pest. Great oxalis, *O. trilliifolia,* is similar but bears two to seven flowers in a raceme. We have six *Oxalis* species, some of them with small yellow flowers.

Poppy Family *(Papaveraceae)*

CALIFORNIA POPPY

Eschscholzia californica. Sometimes turning entire hillsides into blazing orange landscapes, California poppy richly deserves its renown as California's state flower. Each stem in a cluster, 6 to 24 inches high, carries a single saucer-shaped, four-petaled blossom. The petals may vary from 1/3 to 1 1/2 inches long, generally growing smaller as the season progresses. Surmounting the floral stem is a flat receptacle, broader than the flower base, which thus provides a conspicuous rim under the blossom. Sunshine opens the yellow or orange blooms, which close at night or on cloudy days. A bluish, glaucous coating adds an exquisite hue to the linear segments of the thrice-divided, lacy leaves. Most of the leaves originate at the root crown, but a few may attach to the flower stems. Blomming occurs from late spring through summer. HABITAT: Open grassy hills and disturbed areas. RANGE: Southwestern Washington to S California and widely planted elsewhere as an ornamental. COMMENT: Three species of introduced poppies also ocasionally escape from cultivation.

Poppy Family (*Papaveraceae*)

PYGMY POPPY

Papaver pygmaea. From a tuft of basal leaves rise several leafless stems, 1 to 2 1/2 inches tall, crowned with solitary flowers. The arresting, orange-tipped petals shade to yellow at the base. The blossoms expand 1/2 to 3/4 inch wide. Leaf blades are less than 1 inch long and deeply cut into rounded lobes.

Stems, leaves, buds and fruit all bear short, bristly hairs. The plants bloom in midsummer. HABITAT: Rocky talus slopes and cirques. RANGE: Endemic to the Rocky Mountain crest in NW Montana and SW Alberta—mostly in Glacier-Waterton International Peace Park.

Poppy Family (*Papaveraceae*)

CREAM CUPS

Platystemon californicus. This species varies so much that botanists have given it more than 50 different names. The common name cream cups refers to the color of other varieties in California. The annual stem branches from the base, 2 to 12 inches. Creamy white, hairy stamens contrast sharply with the yellow petals of this variety. Bristly hairy, linear leaves grow opposite on the short stems. Spring is blooming time for cream cups. HABITAT: Meadows and open woods from seaside to about 3000 feet elevation. RANGE: Southwestern Oregon to California and Arizona.

Plumbago Family *(Plumbaginaceae)*

Phlox Family *(Polemoniaceae)*

THRIFT, SEA PINK

Armeria maritima. Thrift produces a dense tuft of linear, basal leaves, 2 to 4 inches long. One or more unbranched, naked stems reach 4 to 20 inches high. A tight cluster of rose-colored, tubular flowers, intermixed with sharp-pointed, papery bracts, crowns each stem. Two outer bracts, papery and sometimes purple-hued, reflex sharply downward along the stem. One may find them blooming from spring into midsummer. HABITAT: Sea bluffs or prairies near the sea. RANGE: Circumpolar in the N hemisphere, south to S California.

LARGE FLOWERED COLLOMIA

Collomia grandiflora. This annual may rear simple or sparingly branched stems 1 to 3 feet tall. Each stem tip supports a closely packed head of unusually colored, pale yellow or salmon trumpets, about 1 inch long. Leafy bracts subtend the inflorescence. Narrow, simple leaves attach alternately on the stems. It blooms from late spring into summer. HABITAT: Dry open woods or grassy slopes from valleys to mid elevations in the mountains. RANGE: The Cascades from S British Columbia to California and east to W Montana and Arizona. COMMENT: We have several other species of *Collomia* but not the color of this one.

Phlox Family *(Polemoniaceae)*

Phlox Family *(Polemoniaceae)*

SCARLET GILIA, SKYROCKET

Ipomopsis (Gilia) aggregata. Numerous spectacular trumpets, 3/4 to 1 1/2 inches long, hang on one side of an unbranched stem, 1 to 2 feet tall. Yellow or white speckles commonly embellish the throats of the flowers, which flare into five sharp-pointed petal lobes. The lacy, deeply dissected leaves attach mostly at the base of the plant. Look for these beauties in early summer. HABITAT: Dry grassy hills and plains or among scattered conifers in the mountains. RANGE: Southern Canada to Mexico in the Columbia and Great Basins and in the Rockies.

BLUEFIELD GILIA

Gilia capitata. Round pale blue or darker blue balls *(capitata)*, composed of small trumpet-shaped flowers, unmistakably announce this *Gilia.* From 50 to 100 individual blossoms make up each floral head. The slender annual stems, 6 to 40 inches tall, may or may not branch a few times. The leaves divide twice pinnately into short linear segments. They form a basal rosette as well as sprout on the stem. Look for the blooms in early summer. HABITAT: Dry meadows and slopes at lower elevations. RANGE: From the Cascades westward, S British Columbia to California and in N Idaho. COMMENT: We have two similar species with white flowers: *G. congesta* from central Oregon eastward and south and *G. spicata* from central Idaho east and south.

Phlox Family *(Polemoniaceae)*

SPREADING PHLOX

Phlox diffusa. From a perennial taproot crown spreads a dense cushion of woody stems and leaves, usually not over 4 inches above ground. The leaves are needle-shaped, 1/4 to 3/4 inch long. Solitary, wheel-shaped blossoms terminate many short upright branches, presenting masses of glorious color, ranging from white to pink or blue. Blooms appear in summer. HABITAT: Exposed rocky sites to open forests in the mountains. RANGE: Coastal mountains, British Columbia to California and east to W Montana. COMMENT: Several other species of phlox appear quite similar to this one.

Phlox Family *(Polemoniaceae)*

LONGLEAF PHLOX

Phlox longifolia. From a deep perennial taproot, longleaf phlox spreads several branches, more or less prostrate and woody at the base. Stems can reach 4 to 16 inches in length. The plants vary considerably in leaf size from 1/2 to 3 inches long. They are narrow or linear and attach in opposite pairs at regular nodes on the stems. White to deep pink, fragrant blossoms usually grow in few-flowered, branching clusters. Late spring and early summer for this one. HABITAT: Prairies and open foothills to fairly high montane locations. RANGE: Southern British Columbia to S California, W Montana and New Mexico.

SHOWY PHLOX
Phlox speciosa. This pink or occasionally white phlox spreads five vivid petals that are unmistakably notched or two-lobed on the end. A perennial taproot branches rather profusely into woody stems, 6 to 16 inches in length, that make the plant a semi-shrub. Many linear or lance-shaped leaves, 1 to 3 inches long, grow opposite on the stems. Look for these elegant blooms from April into June. HABITAT: Sagebrush prairies into the mountains. RANGE: South-central British Columbia and E Washington to central and SW Oregon and the Sierras.

Phlox Family *(Polemoniaceae)*

Phlox Family *(Polemoniaceae)*

STICKY PHLOX
Phlox viscida. Sticky phlox closely resembles longleaf phlox, but the plant generally grows smaller and differs in technical features of the calyx. The flowers are pink to purplish or occasionally white, beginning as floral tubes about 1/2 inch long and spreading five rounded lobes about 3/4 to 1 inch across. Pointed, linear leaves grow 1/3 to 1 1/2 inches long and tend to crowd together on stems 2 to 8 inches long. Blooms appear in May and June. HABITAT: Open rocky ridges and slopes. RANGE: Endemic to the Blue Mountains, SE Washington, NE Oregon and adjacent Idaho.

Phlox Family *(Polemoniaceae)*

Phlox Family *(Polemoniaceae)*

JACOB'S LADDER

Polemonium pulcherrimum. These pale blue to purple blossoms open five wide-spreading or shallowly cupped petals and reveal a white or yellow spot in the throat. Typically, white stamens protrude well beyond the petals. The small plants normally do not rise more than 8 inches high. The pinnately compound leaves have about 20 oval leaflets, 1/4 inch long, ranked so uniformly they resemble ladders. They emit a fetid odor, mildly suggestive of skunk, but not particularly noticeable out of doors. Look for Jacob's ladder from May to July. HABITAT: Montane to alpine sites. RANGE: Alaska and the Yukon to N California and Wyoming, excluding the coastal mountains. COMMENT: Another, more robust variety prefers forested habitats at lower elevations.

SKY PILOT

Polemonium viscosum. At the peak of blooming these funnel or bell-shaped flowers, arranged in crowded clusters, simply sparkle in matchless, incredible shades of bluish-purple. Five orange or yellow stamens contrast elegantly with the petals. The plant sends out many branches 6 to 12 inches high. The leaflets of the pinnately compound leaves divide palmately, presenting the appearance of a cascade of tiny leaf whorls. Sticky glandular hairs clothe the leaves and emit an unpleasant odor, somewhat reminiscent of a skunk. Blooming occurs in the summer. HABITAT: Rocky alpine slopes and ridges. RANGE: Eastern Washington to S Alberta and south to New Mexico and Arizona.

Wild Buckwheat Family *(Polygonaceae)*

Wild Buckwheat Family *(Polygonaceae)*

OARLEAF BUCKWHEAT, ARROWLEAF ERIOGONUM

Eriogonum compositum. A clump of many leaves on petioles, 2 to 8 inches long, spreads from a woody taproot. The heart-shaped, arrow-shaped or triangular leaves, green above and hairy white underneath, reliably identify this species of wild buckwheat. Leafless, unbranched flower stems reach 8 to 20 inches high. A compound umbel (twice umbellate) carries many white or yellowish little flowers in a large, tight, headlike inflorescence that is quite showy. Each secondary umbel branch ends in a small hairy cup called an involucre. Numerous tiny blossoms that have only sepals originate in the bottom of the cup on slender stalks. Linear, leaflike bracts subtend both primary and secondary umbels. It blooms from May to July. HABITAT: Prefers rocky hills or cliffs. RANGE: East slope of the Cascades from central Washington to Idaho, south through the Columbia and Great Basins to N California.

CUSHION BUCKWHEAT

Eriogonum ovalifolium var. *depressum.* Cushion buckwheat varies considerably through five varieties, separable mainly on the size and shape of the leaves. In all, the leaves are basal, quite small (1 inch long or less, including the petiole) and beset with woolly, white hairs. The plants often form mats, 12 to 16 inches in diameter. Leafless stems rise 1 to 8 inches above the mats and wear round umbellate heads of tiny cream, yellow or reddish flowers that bloom mostly in summer. HABITAT: Sagebrush prairies to lofty alpine vistas. RANGE: Western North America, British Columbia and Alberta to California and New Mexico.

Wild Buckwheat Family *(Polygonaceae)*

Wild Buckwheat Family *(Polygonaceae)*

STRICT BUCKWHEAT

Eriogonum strictum subspecies *strictum.* This wild buckwheat sends out several to many woody branches about 4 inches long near the ground. Many leaves with oval blades only 1/4 to 1 inch long originate on the branch ends on slender petioles to 4 inches long. The effect is a mat up to 16 inches broad. Numerous leafless floral stems also rise from the branch ends and they branch in turn. Well-spaced involucres create an open inflorescence of white, yellowish or pink to maroon flowers, in which the individual blossoms stand out to better effect than in many of the buckwheats that have tight, headlike flower clusters. May to July for this one. HABITAT: Sagebrush deserts to pine forests. RANGE: East foothills of the Cascades in Washington to Montana, Nevada and NE California. COMMENT: This species has been subdivided into two distinct races or subspecies and several varieties cause wide variations in its appearance.

THYMELEAVED BUCKWHEAT

Eriogonum thymoides. Spreading a foot or more across and 2 to 6 inches high, this many branched, woody shrub develops leaf whorls on branches near the ground and also about mid-height on the upright floral stems. The leaves are short and narrow or linear and quite hairy. Each flower stem, 1 1/2 to 3 1/2 inches tall, supports just one involucre. From a mass of crimson buds appears a tight cluster of white, yellow or reddish flowers that wear hairly coats on the outside. Each plant bears flowers of just one sex, either staminate or pistillate, from April to June. HABITAT: Sagebrush flats to lower mountains. RANGE: Central Oregon and Washington to SW Idaho. COMMENT: Two other species appear very similar to this one: rock buckwheat, *E. sphaerocephalum* and Douglas' buckwheat, *E. douglasii.*

Wild Buckwheat Family *(Polygonaceae)*

WATER SMARTWEED

Polygonum coccineum. Water smartweed parades what appear to be gaudy, unbranched spikes of tiny rose-colored flowers. In reality the inflorescence branches with very short peduncles. The plants produce strong rhizomes that root and send up aerial stems at frequent nodes. The stems may rise to 40 inches and bear many simple, oval and pointed leaves. They bloom from June to September. HABITAT: Partially or wholly aquatic, usually on muddy pond or lake shores to wet soil. RANGE: Most of North America. COMMENT: This species can easily be mistaken for *P. amphibium,* which is also called water smartweed. The two species differ only in technical characters.

Wild Buckwheat Family *(Polygonaceae)*

Purslane Family *(Portulacaceae)*

AMERICAN BISTORT, BOTTLE BRUSH

Polygonum bistortoides. A thick mass of tiny, individual flowers creates cheerful white or reddish heads. Eight stamens protrude from each blossom and impart a ragged, bristly look to the inflorescence. Several slender stems rise 8 to 24 inches from a thick, edible root. Large oblong leaves also shoot up from the root on long petioles. A few small, sessile leaves sheath the stem. Blooming occurs from June to August. HABITAT: Meadows and other moist places from valleys to most commonly alpine regions. RANGE: Western United States and Canada. COMMENT: Very common and frequently abundant, they sometimes turn meadows snowy white.

RED MAIDS

Calandrinia ciliata. This annual herb branches at the base with succulent stems 2 to 12 inches long that spread or lie prostrate on the ground. Many spatula or lance-shaped leaves grow alternate and sessile on the stems. Small but spectacular, dark red to occasional white blossoms grow solitary on the branches, supported by short, flattened peduncles. The flowers bloom from February through springtime. HABITAT: Moist ground, meadows and lawns from the coast to moderate elevations. RANGE: British Columbia to South America, west of the Cascades, but east to Arizona. COMMENT: We have just this one species of *Calandrinia* in the Northwest.

Purslane Family *(Portulacaceae)*

WESTERN SPRING BEAUTY
Claytonia lanceolata. From a nearly round underground corm, similar to a very tiny potato, erupt one or more floral stems, 2 to 8 inches long. Several white to rose, saucer-shaped flowers spread five rounded petals 1/2 to 1 inch in diameter. The petals fuse together at the base in a short tube, have shallow notches at the tip and often show dark red to purple veins on the face. Near the middle, each floral stem bears a pair of linear or lance-shaped *(lanceolata)* leaves. One or more basal leaves may also originate from the corm on long slender petioles. April to July. HABITAT: Wet ground from mountain foothills to high alpine. RANGE: Western Canada and United States.

Purslane Family *(Portulacaceae)*

ALPINE SPRING BEAUTY
Claytonia megarhiza. A large woody root *(megarhiza)* grows nearly 1 inch in diameter and readily identifies this spring beauty. Its favored habitat of loose rocks on steep slopes sometimes moves slowly down hill and the roots elongate with the movement. Many oval or club-shaped leaves sit on long petioles and create a glossy green rosette. Several to many racemes or branching clusters of glistening flowers emerge from under or among the leaves. Look for these exceptional plants in summer. HABITAT: Scree slopes or rock outcrops in alpine terrain. RANGE: Central Washington to S Alberta and south to Nevada and New Mexico.

183

COLUMBIA LEWISIA

Lewisia columbiana. The seductive little flowers of Columbia Lewisia normally possess seven to nine petals, 1/4 to 1/2 inch long, and richly reward the wildflower lover who will seek them out. Crimson to purple veins beautifully mark the white to rose petals. Several slender stems on each plant branch sparingly and produce a many-flowered panicle. The stems reach 4 to 12 inches, usually reclining outward, and both flowers and branches begin in the axils of little bracts with teeth on the margins. The stems, as well as a tuft of narrow, smooth, succulent leaves, 1 to 4 inches long, originate on a fleshy root crown. The blooms appear from late spring to mid-summer, depending on altitude. HABITAT: Rock outcrops or gravelly places in the mountains. RANGE: Coastal mountains to Idaho, S British Columbia to the Sierras. COMMENT: We have six species of *Lewisia* and three varieties of *L. columbiana.*

Purslane Family *(Portulacaceae)*

Purslane Family *(Portulacaceae)*

BITTERROOT

Lewisia rediviva.

Purslane Family *(Portulacaceae)*

BITTERROOT

Lewisia rediviva. One of the most gorgeous wildflowers in our region and the state flower of Montana, bitterroot is now scarce in many areas. About 15 rounded or pointed petals spread 1 1/2 to 3 inches wide. The pale pink to rose or white blossoms appear just above ground line on short stems that rise directly from a deep root crown. Round in cross section, fleshy, and succulent, the leaves also grow from the root, 3/4 to 2 inches long. The leaves begin to wither before the flowers emerge in May and June, sometimes giving the impression that the plants have no life-supporting leaves. HABITAT: Dry prairies to foothill ridges, often on rocky or shallow soil. RANGE: Southern British Columbia to Montana, California and Colorado. COMMENT: Named for Capt. Meriwether Lewis, there are six species of *Lewisia* in the Northwest and nine others to the south. The journals of Lewis and Clark note that Indians dug the roots for food, usually in the spring before they became too bitter to eat.

Purslane Family *(Portulacaceae)*

PIGMY BITTERROOT

Lewisia pygmaea var. *pygmaea*. These exquisite little flowers usually possess seven bright pink, but occasionally white, petals. One or several flower stems rise above or nestle among the rosette of linear, fleshy leaves, which remain through the short growing season. They bloom in midsummer. HABITAT: Gravelly slopes and ridges in subalpine and alpine regions. RANGE: Mountains of W United States and SW Canada. COMMENT: A second variety, *nevadensis*, produces white flowers and dwells at lower elevations in the mountains and foothills.

Purslane Family *(Portulacaceae)*   **Primrose Family** *(Primulaceae)*

PUSSYPAWS

Spraguea umbellata (Calyptridium umbellatum). Arresting, fuzzy heads of tiny pink or white flowers terminate stems that lie prostrate on the ground. On close examination one finds two round, papery and persistent sepals tightly clasping narrower petals that wither early. Some magnification greatly improves one's appreciaton of this intricate flower structure. The unbranched and naked flower stems originate among a rosette of smooth, club-shaped green leaves, 1/2 to 2 inches long. Pussypaws may be annuals at lower elevations and perennials at high altitudes. Blooming occurs from early in the season to midsummer. HABITAT: Sandy or gravelly sites from scattered forest to alpine. RANGE: Southern British Columbia to Montana, Utah and Baja.

ROCK JASMINE

Androsache chamaejasme. From a branching root system, rock jasmine sends short stems horizontally along the ground. A rosette of small simple leaves terminates each stem. Then one vertical flower stalk rises 1 to 4 inches from each rosette. Long silky hairs generously beset the leaves and stalks. An umbel of two to eight small exquisite flowers crowds the tip of each stalk. The creamy blooms, about 1/4 inch in diameter, show bright yellow eyes, blooming in early summer. HABITAT: Gravelly or rocky sites at alpine and subalpine heights. RANGE: An arctic plant of Asia and North America, south through the Rockies to Colorado.

Primrose Family *(Primulaceae)*

Primrose Family *(Primulaceae)*

PRAIRIE SHOOTING STAR

Dodecatheon conjugens. Can anyone fail to stop in awe and wonder at the sight of shooting stars? The sharply reflexed petals that may vary from occasional white to rose or deep magenta, afford a unique, eye-catching design. White or yellow bands usually ring the base of the petals, in this species. The connective tissue between the anthers at the nose of the flower is deeply wrinkled, transversely to the axis of the blossom. The stems support no leaves and reach 4 to 12 inches high. They originate in a rosette of entire leaves that may be smooth or granular (as shown in the photo), depending upon the variety. Mid to late spring for these. HABITAT: Sagebrush prairies into the mountains. RANGE: East slope of the Cascades, British Columbia to California and east to Alberta and Wyoming. COMMENT: We have eight species of shooting star in the Northwest and numerous varieties within the species.

WHITE SHOOTING STAR

Dodecatheon dentatum. This creamy white species normally displays an umbel of two or more blossoms nearly 1 inch long on slender petioles. Five petals cohere at the base in a short tube and then reflex sharply backward from the point of separation. Pale yellow tints ornament the throat where the petals flare. Five maroon or purple anthers form a short tapering cylinder at the nose of the blossom around a style that barely peeks out at the world. Slender, rather succulent stems, 6 to 16 inches tall and naked and unbranched, rise from basal rosettes of leaves. The heart-shaped or oval leaf blades may reach up to 4 inches long and sharp teeth *(dentatum)* serrate their edges. Blooming time is May to July. HABITAT: Rivulets and other wet or moist places under forest shade. RANGE: Mostly the E slope of the Cascades, S British Columbia to N Oregon and scattered to Idaho and N Utah. COMMENT: White sports or albino specimens sometimes occur in other shooting star species.

Primrose Family *(Primulaceae)*

FEW FLOWERED SHOOTING STAR

Dodecatheon pulchellum. This gaudy wildflower looks like a small, colorful rocket. The yellow and purplish-black stamens tightly clasp the style to form the nose, while pink or magenta petals flare backward into a spreading tail. A few flowers in an umbel decorate the top of one or more smooth stems. Several shiny green leaves create a lush basal rosette. This species varies widely and botanists have given it many scientific names. It blooms early in spring at low elevations to midsummer above timberline. HABITAT: Generally damp locations. RANGE: Widespread throughout the West.

Primrose Family *(Primulaceae)*

SMOOTH DOUGLASIA

Douglasia laevigata. Growing in spreading mats or tufts, this hardy perennial reaches only about 2 inches high. Umbels of two to ten flowers on short pedicels crowd the stem tips. The pink to deep magenta or rose-colored blossoms begin as floral tubes, about 1/4 inch long, and then flare five rounded petal lobes widely and reveal a pretty yellow eye in the center. Short, 1/4 to 3/4 inch, narrow leaves make basal whorls or rosettes on woody branches or crowd the branch ends. Blooming can occur from March to August, depending upon altitude and snow melt. HABITAT: Rock outcrops, cliffs or talus slopes. RANGE: Coast to alpine in the Cascades, Washington to N Oregon and the Columbia Gorge. COMMENT: *D. nivalis*, snow douglasia, is endemic to the Wenatchee mountains of Washington.

Primrose Family *(Primulaceae)*

ROCKY MOUNTAIN DOUGLASIA

Douglasia montana. A pretty mass of
pink or rose-colored flowers cover these
cushion plants in spring and early
summer. Rosettes of needle-shaped
leaves about 1/4 inch long support
many short flower stalks. Pistils and
stamens do not project out of the floral
tubes, which have bright yellow throats.

HABITAT: High plains and open foothills
to high mountain ridges. RANGE:
Southwestern Alberta to Idaho and
Wyoming. COMMENT: One could easily
mistake this member of the primrose
family for a *Phlox*, but the lack of
noticeable stamens and pistils helps to
identify it.

Primrose Family *(Primulaceae)*

WESTERN (BROADLEAF) STARFLOWER

Trientalis latifolia. A small forest wraith
raises a simple, delicate stem 3 to 8
inches high from a small tuber deep in
the ground. At the summit of the stem
it holds horizontally a whorl of four to
eight oval or elliptic leaves, 2 to 4
inches long and pointed on the end.
From the axils of these leaves, on

threadlike pedicels, it lifts one to four
star-shaped flowers, composed of four
to seven petals. The white to pink
blossoms open wide about 1/2 inch
across, mostly in springtime. HABITAT:
Occurs commonly in shady woods to
open areas. RANGE: British Columbia to
California, west of the Cascade-Sierra
summit, and to NE Washington and N
Idaho.

191

Buttercup Family *(Ranunculaceae)*

Buttercup Family *(Ranunculaceae)*

MONKSHOOD

Aconitum columbianum. Five showy
sepals set off this extraordinary bloom.
The upper sepal forms a distinctive
hood or helmet with a pointed beak.
Two other fan-shaped sepals spread
wide on the sides and two narrow ones
hang below. In the floral center two or
sometimes five small petals blend with
the sepals and almost disappear
without close scrutiny. Dark blue or
purple flowers predominate, but one
may find a cream-colored variety in E
Oregon and Washington. These tall
plants grow 3 to 7 feet high with broad,
palmately divided and toothed leaves.
They bloom in early summer. HABITAT:
Wet ground or moist woods and forest
fringes from low to subalpine
elevations. RANGE: Forested areas of W
United States and Canada. COMMENT:
Aconitin, a chemical especially prevalent
in the seeds and roots, makes
monkshood very poisonous.

BANEBERRY

Actaea rubra. A tight, nearly spherical
raceme of small white flowers with
many bristling stamens catches the
eye. The tiny, inconspicuous petals
drop off early. This perennial herb
usually branches and bears only a few
very large leaves. The basal leaves
clasp the stem and may branch three
times pinnately. Leaflets in threes have
irregularly toothed margins. Round
berries, either bright waxy red or white
and reportedly poisonous, develop in
mid to late summer. Blooms mostly in
May and June. HABITAT: Moist woods.
RANGE: Most of temperate North
America. COMMENT: Might be
confused with false bugbane, p. 204, or
Hall's rue anemone, p. 201.

192

Buttercup Family *(Ranunculaceae)*

PACIFIC ANEMONE

Anemone multifida. Pacific anemone normally develops a tuft of basal leaves and several upright stems. At mid height each stem produces a whorl of leaves similar to those at the base. From the axils of every whorl usually originate three floral peduncles, each one crowned with a single flower. At least two of the three peduncles commonly carry a whorl of smaller leaves or bracts. Colorful sepals vary from cream to yellow to red, sometimes in combinations of these colors on one plant. They bloom from early in the season to August. HABITAT: Open slopes and rocky places from medium elevations to alpine. RANGE: The cold regions of the Americas from the arctic to the Straits of Magellan. COMMENT: We have three varieties of Pacific anemone and two other species that resemble this one.

Buttercup Family *(Ranunculaceae)*

Buttercup Family *(Ranunculaceae)*

BLUE ANEMONE, OREGON WINDFLOWER

Anemone oregana. This delicate little plant sends up a simple stem, 4 to 10 inches high. Spreading from rhizomes, it creates open colonies. The normally blue blossom spreads five to eight oval sepals, 1 to 1 1/2 inches across. It has no true petals. Beneath the single flower a whorl of three palmately compound leaves attaches with three to five lobes each, that in turn are irregularly toothed on the margins. An occasional three-lobed leaf will sprout from the rhizome without giving rise to a flower. It blooms in spring. HABITAT: Moist woods or forest openings at upper elevations. RANGE: East slope of the Cascades to the coast. COMMENT: A variety, *felix,* prefers sphagnum bogs near the coast and produces lavender, pink or white blooms. Lyall's anemone, *A. lyallii,* resides from the Cascades to the coast and bears mostly blue flowers.

WINDFLOWER

Anemone piperi. Windflower normally deploys five showy sepals, but sometimes one finds a "double" with ten sepals. These lovely white or delicate pink anemones provide a tonic for the spirits soon after spring arrives. A mound of greenish stamens decorates the center of the blossom. Three leaves in a whorl, each with three toothed leaflets, encircle the stem just below the flower. Look for these gay jewels from April to June. HABITAT: Woodsy canyon bottoms and damp forests. RANGE: Eastern Oregon and Washington to W Montana.

RED COLUMBINE, SITKA COLUMBINE

Aquilegia formosa. The flowers of this captivating columbine display five petals with broad, yellow, rounded blades flaring in front and tapering to straight, brick red spurs about 1/2 inch long, extending backward. The petals attach near the middle to a ring of sepals, also brick red, which alternate with the petals and spread wide or curve backward. A multitude of stamens protrude from the nodding blossoms. Mostly basal leaves divide three times into threes, the leaflets cleft into irregular, rounded lobes. A few much-reduced leaves also affix to the stems, which stand 6 to 40 inches or so tall. Blooming can occur from May through August. HABITAT: Highly variable from seashore to subalpine. RANGE: Alaska to Baja, Montana and Utah.

Buttercup Family *(Ranunculaceae)*

Buttercup Family *(Ranunculaceae)*

TWINFLOWER MARSH MARIGOLD

Caltha biflora. Twinflower marsh marigold produces a tuft of basal leaves and one flowering stem that reaches 6 inches or less before branching. The stem branches just once into two peduncles that usually reach 6 to 12 inches higher. A single small stem leaf sprouts at the branch and a solitary flower tops each peduncle (biflora). Each blossom has seven to twelve white or creamy sepals. The round or broadly heart-shaped, succulent leaves normally reveal tiny rounded scallops on the margins. May into August. HABITAT: Wet meadows and streambanks. RANGE: Alaska to W Montana, California and Colorado. COMMENT: *C. leptosepala*, produces just one flower per plant.

Buttercup Family *(Ranunculaceae)*   **Buttercup Family** *(Ranunculaceae)*

YELLOW (GOLDEN) COLUMBINE

Aquilegia flavescens. This elegant
columbine normally supports several to
many flowers exhibiting two delicate
shades of yellow, but reddish coloration
can occur that is very similar to red
columbine. Five petals attach in the
middle to simple sepals and alternate
with them. In front, rounded petal lobes
open wide and taper into spurs behind.
The spurs reach about 1/2 inch long or
more and they curl inward at the end.
Nectar in the spurs can only be reached
by long tongues of hummingbirds, moths
and butterflies. The plants grow 3 to 30
inches tall. Robust plants usually branch
several times, but some dwarfed alpine
specimens may have only simple stems.
A few reduced stem leaves or bracts
always occur, even on the smallest
plants. A few compound basal leaves
divide into three leaflets that are three-
lobed in turn, thin and mostly lie flat. A
late spring and early summer bloomer.
HABITAT: Meadows and moist woods
from montane to alpine scree slopes and
cirques. RANGE: Southwestern Canada,
Washington Cascades and south to Utah
and Colorado.

STANDLEY'S COLUMBINE

Aquilegia X elatior (Hybrid). In his "Flora
of Glacier National Park, Montana"
Standley describes this columbine as a
variety of Jones columbine, standing 4 to
8 inches tall. Later floras simply expand
the description of *Aq. jonesii* to include
this one. I have observed it in several
locations, standing 3 to 12 inches tall,
always in close proximity to both *Aq.
jonesii* and *Aq. flavescens.* I believe it is
a hybrid of these two species. Furthermore, I have observed almost a complete progression of color phases and
other plant characteristics from one
parent to the other. The blue and pale
yellow flowers grow spurs about 3/8
inch long that may either be straight or
somewhat incurling. The leaves are in-
termediate between the two progenitors.
Standley's columbine also may bear
more than one flower per stem. Even
with only one blossom, it always carries
a floral stem leaf or bract, apparently a
contribution from *Aq. flavescens* and different from typical Jones columbine. It
blooms in July or early August. HABITAT:
Limestone scree at alpine heights.
RANGE: The Rocky Mountain front, SW
Alberta and Montana.

Buttercup Family (Ranunculaceae)

JONES COLUMBINE, LIMESTONE COLUMBINE

Aquilegia jonesii. Rare but not endangered, the bloom of this indescribably blue or purplish columbine compares favorably in size with the other species. The spurs are straight and extend backward only about 1/4 inch. Each flower rests solitary on a short, unbranched stem that does not bear any stem leaves or bracts. The plants grow in a tuft or small mat only 2 to 4 inches high in a mass of very small hairy leaves that divide three times into threes. Many small, oval, somewhat leathery leaflets crowd each other and overlap conspicuously so they do not lie flat. It blooms mostly in late June and early July. HABITAT: Restricted to limestone scree slopes, ridge tops or outcrops above timberline. RANGE: Sporadic along the Rocky Mountain crest from S Alberta to Wyoming. COMMENT: Jones columbine will flourish only in its preferred habitat and does not long survive transplanting. Enjoy it in its lofty native home and leave it for others to savor.

Buttercup Family *(Ranunculaceae)*   Buttercup Family *(Ranunculaceae)*

PURPLE VIRGIN'S BOWER, BLUE CLEMATIS

Clematis columbiana. Rather short, woody vines creep along the ground or climb on shrubs or other supports when available. The regal blue or purple flowers possess four or sometimes five pointed sepals, 1 1/2 to 2 1/2 inches long, that bow or nod modestly for the mountain visitor. A mass of stamens and pistils make a white or greenish yellow mound in the center of the blossom. The flowers terminate rather long bare peduncles. Compound leaves possess three widely spaced, lance-shaped leaflets that usually show indentations but no lobes on the edges. However, a variety endemic to the Wenatchee mountains of Washington does develop strongly lobed leaflets. They bloom from May to July. HABITAT: Open areas and mid elevation woods to near alpine. RANGE: British Columbia, east of the Cascades, and Alberta to Oregon and Wyoming. COMMENT: Two other species relate closely to this one, but they both bear deeply lobed leaflets.

WESTERN WHITE CLEMATIS, VIRGINSBOWER

Clematis ligusticifolia. These climbing, woody vines often cover fences, shrubs and small trees. The flowers have five or six sepals but no petals and normally open less than 1 inch across. The pinnately compound leaves have five to seven irregularly toothed leaflets. Blooming occurs in late spring and early summer. HABITAT: Valleys and sagebrush plains to forest margins, where the soil is fairly deep and moist. RANGE: Central British Columbia to Alberta and south to California and New Mexico. COMMENT: In fruit, masses of silvery plumes develop. The styles persist on small, hairy seeds, elongate to 1 to 2 inches and develop feathery hairs.

Buttercup Family *(Ranunculaceae)*

Buttercup Family *(Ranunculaceae)*

SUGARBOWL

Clematis hirsutissima. Spectacular but modestly nodding, cup- or bell-shaped flowers may show pale or dark purple coloration on the outside and normally dark blue or purple inside. A mass of tempting yellow stamens fills the throat of the cup. One may easily overlook these extraordinary flowers in a clump of large deeply divided or lacy leaves. Several stems 1 to 2 feet high wear a dense coat of woolly hairs *(hirsutissima)* that may also cover the flower exterior. The floral stems support solitary, terminal blossoms. They bloom in spring. HABITAT: Grassy prairies to scattered woods. RANGE: Southern British Columbia to Montana, central Oregon and Wyoming.

LITTLE LARKSPUR, MONTANA LARKSPUR

Delphinium bicolor. This showy perennial displays several irregular blue flowers on a simple stem, 3 to 15 inches tall. Five stylish, widespreading sepals attract immediate attention. The upper sepal extends backward forming a long conical spur. The four petals are much smaller than the sepals. An upper pair shows white with blue lines. A lower pair, dark blue and inconspicuous, blends in with the sepals. Leaves are palmately compound and deeply parted into slender leaflets. Blooms in springtime. HABITAT: Grassy prairies to scattered coniferous forest. RANGE: Eastern Washington to Saskatchewan, South Dakota and Wyoming. COMMENT: Some authors call low species larkspurs and tall species delphinium, while others consider annuals to be the larkspurs and perennials delphinium. In scientific nomenclature they are all *Delphinium.*

Buttercup Family *(Ranunculaceae)*

COLUMBIA DELPHINIUM (LARKSPUR)

Delphinium trolliifolium. Rising 2 1/2 to 5 feet tall, Columbia delphinium sends up several hollow stems from a tough woody root. The stems, simple below, may or may not branch in the inflorescence. Palmate leaves, cleft deeply into five or seven lobes, attach at regular nodes along the stem and grow smaller upward. In addition, large sharp teeth serrate the leaf margins. Near the base the leaf blades may spread 4 to 8 inches across and rest on long petioles. The irregular flowers display five large, dark blue, showy sepals. Four smaller petals sit in the center of the blossom, two dark blue below and two white ones above. Look for this impressive plant in mid to late spring. HABITAT: Wet places in deep forests. RANGE: Southwestern Washington, the Columbia Gorge and the western slope of the Cascades to N California. COMMENT: We have about 18 species of *Delphinium* in the Pacific Northwest.

Buttercup Family *(Ranunculaceae)*

Buttercup Family *(Ranunculaceae)*

UPLAND LARKSPUR

Delphinium nuttallianum. This low, perennial *Delphinium* varies considerably through five varieties in the northwest. In general the plants send up just one stem, 4 to 16 inches tall, that supports a more or less open raceme of flowers. The dark blue to occasional white blossoms display five spreading sepals, the upper one protruding backward into a spur 1/2 to 1 inch long. Four smaller petals decorate the floral center, two above, rounded and often white with dark blue veins and two dark ones below, deeply cleft into lobes. Palmately divided leaves rise mostly from the base, but a few smaller leaves may attach on the stem. They bloom in spring and early summer. HABITAT: Rocky or gravelly prairies and foothills to scattered ponderosa pine forests. RANGE: Southern British Columbia and Alberta, east of the Cascades to N California, Nebraska and Arizona.

HALL'S RUE ANEMONE

Isopyrum hallii. In bloom rue anemone presents eye-catching, flat-topped clusters (umbels or near umbels) of white blooms. A flower normally possesses five oval, wide-spreading sepals, white or tinged with rose or purple. Above the sepals stands a mass of pure white, upright stamens. On close inspection the filaments supporting the anthers of the stamens are not round but flattened and widest near the top. Normally the plant sends up a single stem 1 1/2 to 2 1/2 feet tall, with only three leaves that grow smaller upward. The petiole of the basal leaf branches twice pinnately and the leaflets, triangular in outline, are cleft irregularly into three main lobes that in turn have irregular rounded teeth on the end. Blooming takes place in midsummer. HABITAT: Moist shady woods. RANGE: Southwestern Washington, Columbia Gorge and the N Willamette Valley. COMMENT: Rue anemone could be mistaken for false bugbane, p. 204, or baneberry, p. 192, but its limited range prevents confusion over much of the ranges of the latter two species.

Buttercup Family *(Ranunculaceae)*

ALPINE BUTTERCUP

Ranunculus eschscholtzii. These smooth, perky little plants display one to three blossoms each. Several or many of them often grow in masses on favorable sites. Five waxy, yellow petals and numerous yellow or green stamens adorn each flower. Most of the glossy green leaves spring from the base of the plants on slender petioles. They spread three palmate lobes, parted more than half way to the base, and the lobes may be roundly scalloped. Look for these beauties in early summer. HABITAT: Wet places in alpine terrain. RANGE: Mountains of W North America, north of Mexico.

Buttercup Family *(Ranunculaceae)*

CREEPING BUTTERCUP

Ranunculus flammula. Spreading by means of runners, this creeping buttercup roots by layering at frequent leaf nodes. A mass of slender roots creates a shallow fibrous web just below the surface of the ground. Small yellow flowers, 1/3 to 1/2 inch across, rise singly at nodes near stem ends. Simple leaves attach in pairs at the nodes—those near the base of the plant on petioles and those farther away from the base sessile. It blooms from May to July. HABITAT: Wet sand or brackish mud from sea coast into foothills and lower mountains. RANGE: Western North America, across Canada and along the Atlantic coast and in Europe.

Buttercup Family (Ranunculaceae)

SAGEBRUSH BUTTERCUP

Ranunculus glaberrimus. Schoolchildren throughout the West search for the first wildflowers of spring and, more often than not, find sagebrush buttercup. The waxy, shiny, yellow cups have five, or as many as eight petals. A small pocket at the base of each petal holds nectar for bees and other pollinating insects. Many yellow stamens encircle a mound of greenish yellow pistils in the center of the blossom. Five shorter sepals beneath the petals wear a purplish tinge. Several stems usually spring from fleshy roots and reach 2 to 8 inches. Most of the leaves attach at the base on long petioles. The round or oval and fleshy leaf blades may be either simple or three-lobed, and both kinds often occur on each plant. HABITAT: Prairies and foothills to piney woods. RANGE: Much of W North America. COMMENT: One can find more than 40 species of buttercup in our area.

WESTERN MEADOWRUE

Thalictrum occidentale. This species has male (staminate) flowers and female (pistillate) flowers on separate plants. One more easily notices the male flowers, which consist of masses of pendulous yellow stamens, about 1/8 inch long, hanging on slender, brownish purple filaments as shown in the photo. Small papery sepals (no petals) make tiny umbrellas above the flowers. The female flowers are inconspicuous, green or purplish, burr-like heads of naked ovaries (upper left in the photo). Large leaves clasp the stem at the base and divide or branch two to four times. Shiny leaflets, about 1 inch across, are rounded and normally three-lobed. The lobes in turn have rounded scallops. May to July. HABITAT: Woods and meadows. RANGE: Cascades and Rockies, south to Colorado and N California.

Buttercup Family (Ranunculaceae)

Buttercup Family *(Ranunculaceae)*

Buttercup Family *(Ranunculaceae)*

FALSE BUGBANE

Trautvetteria caroliniensis. Flat-topped masses of showy, greenish white flowers perch on top of stems 1 1/2 to 3 feet tall. Each blossom has four or more small linear sepals and numerous stamens about 1/4 inch long. The attractive leaves are palmately lobed, like maple leaves, 4 to 10 inches broad and toothed on the margins. They sprout mostly from the base of the plant. Blooms appear from May to July. HABITAT: Damp ground in the woods. RANGE: British Columbia to Montana, New Mexico and California; central and E United States and Japan. COMMENT: Widely scattered but not very common in our region. See baneberry, p. 192, and Hall's rue anemone, p. 201.

GLOBEFLOWER

Trollius laxus. This memorable plant sends up several stems in a clump, 4 to 12 inches high. A solitary flower, about 1 1/2 inches in diameter, terminates each stem and consists of five or more white, cream or pale yellow sepals. In the northern part of its range, white flowers predominate while pale yellow ones occur more commonly to the south. Numerous yellow stamens embellish the center. Minute linear petals form a ring around the stamens and usually go unnoticed. The leaves divide palmately into five lobes, each one further lobed irregularly. Three leaves normally attach to each stem, the upper one closely subtending the flower that opens soon after snow melt. HABITAT: Wet woods, meadows and stream banks, subalpine and alpine. RANGE: British Columbia and Alberta, south to Washington and Colorado. Also rare in NE states, Michigan to Connecticut.

Peony Family *(Paeoniaceae)*

BROWN'S PEONY

Paeonia brownii Closely related to the buttercup family, a large, spellbinding flower, 3 to 4 inches across, sits at the end of a stem 8 to 24 inches long. Several large leaves alternate on the stem. They divide once or twice pinnately and deep lobes cut the leaflets, covered with a waxy, glaucous coat. The heavy, fleshy succulent blossoms often bend the stems over, sometimes to the ground. Each flower has an outer ring of five or six oval, leathery sepals, green or reddish-colored. A second ring of five to ten slightly longer petals varies from white to maroon, purple or bronze, often rimmed with bright yellow. A multitude of stamens encircle a prominent, five-parted, superior green ovary. Late spring for this one. HABITAT: Sagebrush prairies into the mountains. RANGE: Central Washington to Idaho, south to NW Wyoming, Utah and the Sierras. COMMENT: Our only peony native to North America, but a California variety is sometimes classed as a separate species.

Buckthorn Family *(Rhamnaceae)*

Buckthorn Family *(Rhamnaceae)*

DEERBRUSH, BUCKBRUSH

Ceanothus integerrimus. Adding
considerably to the fragrance of
springtime breezes, the many tiny
flowers of deerbrush create white to
blue or lavender, conical clusters on the
ends of thin flexible twigs. This
branching shrub may grow 3 to 15 feet
tall. Elliptic to lance-shaped leaves about
2 inches long show three prominent
veins. The flowers, which resemble
small lilacs from a distance, bloom
profusely in May and June. HABITAT:
Prefers open brushy forest slopes or
roadsides. RANGE: East slope of the
Cascades in Washington, moving farther
west to the coast in SW Oregon, and
south to New Mexico and Baja.

SNOWBRUSH

Ceanothus velutinus. This squat,
sprawling, many-branched shrub grows
1 1/2 to 8 feet tall. Its oval, leathery,
evergreen leaves, 2 to 4 inches long,
have sticky, shiny-green upper surfaces
and light colored under sides. The
leaves grow alternate near stem ends,
have very fine teeth on the margins
and show three prominent veins. Tight,
rounded clusters of tiny white flowers
make showy, strongly scented blooms
in the summer. HABITAT: Forest
openings and fringes. RANGE: British
Columbia to South Dakota and south to
central California and Colorado.
COMMENT: Snowbrush seeds are
impervious to moisture and require
heat or scarification to germinate.
Following forest fires it may regenerate
strongly in areas where it was not
previously in evidence, leading to
speculation that its seeds had lain in
the forest duff for perhaps 300 years
or more, dating back to a previous fire.
Shade from subsequent forest trees
had then eliminated the plant from the
forest understory, until another fire
happened.

Buckthorn Family *(Rhamnaceae)*

SQUAW CARPET

Ceanothus prostratus. Squaw carpet makes excellent ground cover in shady places, a creeping shrub spreading its mat up to 9 feet in diameter. On the hairy young stems, pairs of opposite, evergreen leaves erupt from regularly occurring nodes. The oblong leaves, about 1 inch long, possess prominent, sharp teeth on the edges, somewhat resembling holly leaves. Short, lateral stems arising from the leaf axils support clusters (corymbs) of tiny, off-white to pink or, more commonly, pale blue flowers from May to July. HABITAT: Well-drained forests, usually pine. RANGE: East slope of the Cascades in Washington to W Nevada and the Sierras.

Buckthorn Family *(Rhamnaceae)*

CASCARA BUCKTHORN

Rhamnus purshiana. Once sought after for commercial use, the bark of this shrub affords reliable laxative compounds. Its occurrence in our flora has been reduced by harvesting in the past for medicinal use. It branches sparingly and grows upright to 30 feet tall. Short petioles support oval leaf blades, 2 to 6 inches long. The leaves show prominent parallel veins and tiny sharp teeth on the margins. The yellowish green flowers, about 1/8 inch long, grow in umbels in the axils of upper leaves. In the fall, dark purple berries replace the flowers. It blooms in spring. HABITAT: Open stream banks to forest understory at low to moderate elevations. RANGE: British Columbia to N California, Montana and NE Oregon.

Rose Family *(Rosaceae)*

SERVICEBERRY, SHADBUSH

Amelanchier alnifolia. This common shrub produces short racemes of five-petaled, white or occasionally pinkish flowers. The showy petals, about 1/2 to 3/4 inch long, may spread wide or curl backward. They emerge from the edge of a flat cup that becomes a navy blue berry (actually a pome) as the fruit ripens. Indians used the seedy, rather insipid berries extensively for making pemmican. The oval leaves, 1 to 2 inches long; vary from smooth on the edges to finely toothed. They bloom from April into summer. HABITAT: Open hillsides to rather dense forest, low to subalpine elevations. RANGE: Western North America, north of Mexico. COMMENT: Serviceberry varies considerably through five recognized varieties. In addition, Utah serviceberry, a smaller shrub occupies the Great Basin from S Oregon and Idaho southward and eastward. Big game animals relish all parts of the plant and birds and small animals eat the berries, especially in winter.

Rose Family *(Rosaceae)*

GOAT'S BEARD

Aruncus sylvester. Several arresting sprays of tiny white flowers cover the branches of a panicle to 20 inches long. This strong, perennial herb sends up several stems, 3 to 6 feet, that tend to sag from the weight of the inflorescences. The leaves attach to the stems and grow smaller near the top. Pinnately compound (twice pinnate near the base) the lance-shaped leaflets have sharp serrations on the margins with smaller teeth on the edges of the major serrations. Blooming is late spring to early summer. HABITAT: Wet places in the woods. RANGE: Boreal forests of the N hemisphere, including Japan; Alaska to N California in the Coast and Cascade ranges.

Rose Family *(Rosaceae)*

BLACK (RIVER) HAWTHORN

Crataegus douglasii (Crataegus rivularis). Stout thorns about 1 inch long arm this large, spreading shrub or small tree. The flowers usually have five rounded, white petals and 10 to 20 stamens. They create showy clusters on branch ends and in leaf axils. Small, dry, seedy apples, called haws, develop in the fall. Birds and small animals feed on them in winter. The flowers appear in May and June. HABITAT: Stream banks, prairies and open woods with deep soil. RANGE: Southern Alaska to Alberta, California and Colorado. COMMENT: Black hawthorn provides the preferred nesting habitat for magpies.

Rose Family *(Rosaceae)*

WHITE MOUNTAIN AVENS, DRYAD
(See description on facing page.)

Rose Family *(Rosaceae)*

WHITE MOUNTAIN AVENS, DRYAD

Dryas octopetala. Each flower of this low, mat-forming semishrub normally displays eight petals *(octopetala)* and many yellow stamens. The white flowers open about 1 1/2 inches wide and perch slightly above or nestle among the leaves. The evergreen leaves grow about 1 inch long, elliptic in shape, and exhibit scallops on the surface between prominent veins and edges that curl under. Although bright green above, silvery hairs generously coat the undersides. Look for them in early summer. HABITAT: Common on the highest windswept slopes and mountain tops, they also occur on gravel bars at subalpine altitudes. RANGE: Arctic regions of the northern hemisphere, south to Washington and Colorado. COMMENT: In fruit the styles persist as feathery tails that help the wind carry the seeds. Orange earth star lichen (p. 210) makes a colorful contrast in the alpine environment.

Rose Family *(Rosaceae)*

BEACH STRAWBERRY

Fragaria chiloensis. This wild strawberry sprouts numerous, distinctive, three-bladed leaves that all originate at the root crown. They have shiny, dark green, wrinkled upper surfaces, marked with prominent veins, grayish and hairy underneath. Reddish and quite hairy stolons or runners enable the plants to spread and create large patches. Five round white petals surround a bright yellow mound of pistils and stamens. Five to fifteen flowers in a branching inflorescence form a cyme. The blooms show up in spring and early summer. HABITAT: Ocean beaches, sand dunes and bluffs. RANGE: Alaska to central California, South America and Hawaii.

PRAIRIE SMOKE, PURPLE AVENS

Geum triflorum. One to several, but usually three, top-shaped flowers nod gracefully in the prairie breeze. They are brick red, rosy or yellowish with red stripes. The outer sepals nearly hide the light yellow petals. The fruit become puffs of long, feathery plumes that are carried on the wind. The leaves divide into many segments. Blooming occurs early in the spring or into summer at high elevations. HABITAT: Open prairie and foothills where the soil is quite deep and moist in the spring to meadows above timberline. RANGE: The northern third of the continental U.S. east of the Cascades and much of Canada.

Rose Family *(Rosaceae)*

Rose Family *(Rosaceae)*

OCEAN SPRAY, MOUNTAIN SPRAY

Holodiscus discolor. Cascading masses of upright or mostly pendulous, creamy white flower clusters remind one of waves breaking on the ocean shore. The tiny, individual flowers, arranged in panicles, have five petals. Very common in our region, ocean spray, the shrub, branches many times from below ground as well as above and reaches up to 15 feet tall. The slender reddish shoots show prominent ribs in the bark and bend over from the weight of the heavy flower sprays, especially on older plants. Dried, brown flower clusters remain on the plants through winter and provide seeds for birds and small animals. Alternate, oval leaf blades reach 1 1/2 to 3 inches, wear silvery hairy coats below and show shallow lobes that in turn have coarse teeth on the margins. Blooms in summer.
HABITAT: Open areas to woodlands from the coast into the mountains.
RANGE: British Columbia to Montana, NE Oregon and S California.
COMMENT: A shorter species with smaller leaves, *H. dumosus*, prefers the drier regions of the Great Basin.

Rose Family *(Rosaceae)*

Rose Family *(Rosaceae)*

PARTRIDGEFOOT

Luetkea pectinata. Occasionally one encounters a wildflower so captivating that the memory lingers long after many others are forgotten. Partridgefoot can cast such a spell for the alpine hiker. The tiny, white flowers form a tight cluster atop a 2 to 6 inch stem. Yellow eyes gleam from the floral centers. The leaves, deeply parted into linear segments remind one of birds tracks in the dust or snow. They sometimes create dense mats, since the plants spread by stolons, usually on fairly deep soil. Search for this choice alpine in summer. HABITAT: Meadows and slopes, often in snow retention areas, subalpine and alpine. RANGE: Alaska to Idaho, Montana and N California. COMMENT: *Luetkea* has just one species.

SQUAW APPLE

Peraphyllum ramosissimum. This admirable shrub sprays its branches outward like a fountain. It reaches 2 to 6 feet tall and has pink to rose "apple" blossoms about 1/2 inch across. The five wide-spreading petals frame a mass of stamens and styles. Furthermore, the leaves cluster on short spurs in the manner of apples. There the resemblance ends, because the leaves, 1/2 to 1 1/2 inches long, are simple and end in a short point. The fruit is a very small, yellow or reddish pome with a bitter taste. It blooms in May and June. HABITAT: Sagebrush prairie to foothills and open piny woods. RANGE: Eastern Oregon and S Idaho to E California and W Colorado.

Rose Family *(Rosaceae)*

NINEBARK

Physocarpus malvaceus. Tight, round clusters of white, five-petaled flowers, brownish yellow in the center, radiate many stamens and decorate this choice shrub. In autumn the flowers turn into brown seed husks. The bushes grow to 6 feet, branch prolifically and sometimes effect dense thickets. Grayish bark seemingly shreds and peels continuously on older stems. Young stems bear many star-shaped hair clusters, which require magnification for full appreciation. Three- or five-lobed, alternate leaves show many sharp teeth on the margins and remind one of maple leaves. The blooms appear in early summer. HABITAT: Canyons and rocky foothills to fairly dense Douglas fir and ponderosa pine forests. RANGE: East of the Cascades, British Columbia to Alberta, central Oregon, Utah and Wyoming. COMMENT: *Physocarpus capitatus* grows to 12 feet tall and stays west of the Cascades from Alaska to California, except for a small population in N Idaho.

Rose Family *(Rosaceae)*

Rose Family *(Rosaceae)*

SHRUBBY CINQUEFOIL, POTENTILLA

Potentilla fruticosa. Called "potentilla" by the nursery trade, this native shrub has become a commonly planted ornamental. The handsome plants grow 1 to 4 feet tall and bear solitary flowers about 1 inch across, or small clusters in leaf axils. Five broad petals radiate outward from a mass of similarly colored stamens. The pinnate leaves usually consist of five narrow or linear leaflets about 1/2 inch long. Silky hairs impart a gray-green cast to the leaves. The blossoms first appear in early summer. HABITAT: Open woods and meadows in the mountains to alpine heights. RANGE: Cold, mostly mountainous regions of the N hemisphere.

PACIFIC SILVERWEED

Potentilla pacifica. Spreading by aerial runners that root where nodes touch the ground, this species resembles strawberries in this respect. The feathery leaves have from nine to thirty-one oval leaflets, 1/2 to 1 1/2 inches long, pinnately arranged, that display many sharp "shark's" teeth on the edges. The longer leaves may reach 16 inches in length. Bright green above, the leaflets sometimes grow silvery hairs underneath. Single flowers arise from the leaf nodes on the runners near the base of the plant. Each blossom, 3/4 to 1 1/4 inches in diameter and supported on a slender peduncle, has five yellow petals that may shade to orange at the base. This one blooms in late spring and early summer. HABITAT: Coastal sand dunes and sandy flats. RANGE: Alaska to S California. COMMENT: A very similar species, common silverweed, *P. anserina*, occurs throughout most of North America, east of the Cascade-Sierras.

Rose Family *(Rosaceae)*

Rose Family *(Rosaceae)*

BITTER CHERRY

Prunus emarginata. Bitter cherry is normally a small tree to 45 feet high in the western part of its range, but more commonly a poorly formed shrub, 6 to 20 feet tall, east of the Cascades. It has reddish bark on the twigs. The white flowers form rounded branching clusters near twig ends and project numerous stamens. The fruit, a single-seeded, black drupe, has a very bitter flavor. Oval leaves have tiny teeth on the margins and rounded or obtuse ends. It blooms from April to June. HABITAT: Open prairie or moist woods from low elevations to subalpine. RANGE: British Columbia to S California, Montana and Arizona.

CHOKECHERRY

Prunus virginiana. A round columnar mass of pleasing white flowers decorates a shrub or small tree and identifies chokecherry. Small teeth serrate the edges of oval or elliptical leaves, 2 to 4 inches long. The small, seedy cherries, dark red to black when ripe, have a bitter taste that is not altogether unpalatable after the first one! Makes gourmet jam or jelly. Blooms in late spring and early summer. HABITAT: Open valleys, foothills and watercourses. RANGE: Temperate North America. COMMENT: We have two varieties in the Northwest and several others are recognized elsewhere.

Rose Family *(Rosaceae)*

Rose Family *(Rosaceae)*

ANTELOPE BRUSH, BITTERBRUSH

Purshia tridentata. This spreading, many-branched shrub stands 2 to 10 feet tall. Distinctive leaves grow less than 1 inch long and have three small, rounded lobes on the ends. The branches typically grow many stubby side shoots, which bear solitary flowers. The blossoms feature five yellow petals and many stamens. After a brief blooming period in the spring, the petals fall off early. HABITAT: Dry hills and plains into the fringes of ponderosa pine forests. RANGE: Western United States and Canada, east of the Cascades. COMMENT: Named for Frederick Pursh, the botanist who first catalogued the plant specimens collected by Lewis and Clark. Game animals such as deer and antelope often browse on antelope brush.

PRICKLY ROSE

Rosa acicularis. Prickly rose, the floral emblem of Alberta, closely resembles Wood's rose, but differs mainly in the prickles. The spines grow slender, straight, and numerous and often vary in length. They occur along both twigs and older stems. The plants reach 1 to 5 feet high and the leaves normally have five or seven oval leaflets, toothed on the edges. All of our native roses have stipules, or bracts at the base of the leaves, that adhere to the leaf rachis for much of their length. In fruit the edible but seedy hips turn bright red and the sepals persist on the ends. Blooming time is June to August. HABITAT: Mostly a forest understory shrub. RANGE: The N hemisphere in boreal forests, south to British Columbia, Idaho, Montana and New Mexico.

WOOD'S ROSE, WILD ROSE
Rosa woodsii. Five beautiful pink to dark rose petals surround a mound of yellow stamens and pistils. Wood's rose generally has two stout thorns at the base of each leaf and sometimes some weaker prickles between the nodes. Mostly the thorns grow straight, but some may curve and some have thick bases. The leaflets, oval in outline, reach up to 2 inches long and 1 inch wide, and sharp teeth line the edges. Blooms appear from May to July. HABITAT: Prefers moist woods and stream banks in the mountains. RANGE: North-central Canada to S California, east of the Cascade summit and east to Wisconsin and Missouri.

Rose Family *(Rosaceae)*

Rose Family *(Rosaceae)*

THIMBLEBERRY
Rubus parviflorus. These common shrubs grow in patches, spreading from underground roots. The stems usually rise 2 to 4 feet and do not branch below the crown. The inflorescence branches ordinarily, bearing three or four blossoms or a few more. Broad, palmately lobed leaves dwarf the white or occasionally pink flowers. The red, raspberry-like fruit has a mealy, insipid taste. They bloom from May to July. HABITAT: Low to high in the mountains in scattered to dense forest. RANGE: Alaska to Mexico and east to the Great Lakes.

Rose Family *(Rosaceae)*

SALMONBERRY

Rubus spectabilis. A near relative of raspberries, the woody canes grow straight or curved, 3 to 12 feet tall. They spread under ground by rhizomes and in favorable locations can make dense thickets. Many prickles guard the canes near the bottom but become sparse higher up. Pink to magenta flowers, about 1 inch wide, occur singly or a few in a cluster on side branches. The leaves produce three or five pinnate leaflets, which display large teeth and have smaller serrations on their margins. Rather large, rounded berries show yellowish orange (salmon) or red coloration—edible but not very sweet. They bloom early in the season into summer. HABITAT: Wet ground of woods and stream banks. RANGE: Alaska to NW California, the coast to the W Cascades.

Rose Family *(Rosaceae)*

PACIFIC (TRAILING) BLACKBERRY

Rubus ursinus. Trailing vines ramble 15 to 18 feet along the ground and root by layering at the end. The vines bear vicious, backward curving spines. The leaves, double toothed on the margins, have mostly three lobes. The white petals about 1/2 inch long surround a mound of many stamens on the unisexual flowers shown. Sweet, juicy blackberries grow about 1 inch long. The plants bloom early in summer. HABITAT: Prairies to forests and logged areas, from the coast to mid elevations in the mountains. RANGE: British Columbia to Idaho and N California. COMMENT: We have just this one species of native blackberry in the Northwest.

Rose Family *(Rosaceae)*

CASCADE MOUNTAIN ASH

Sorbus scopulina. A multitude of tiny, white flowers create dense, flat-topped clusters to 6 inches broad on branch ends of this strong shrub. Bright orange berries replace the flowers in the fall. The leaves have 9 to 13 pinnate leaflets, pointed on the end and sharply toothed. This aesthetic shrub often forms dense thickets. Blooming occurs in early summer. HABITAT: Steep mountainsides, woods and cut-over land. RANGE: Alaska to Alberta, New Mexico and N California. COMMENT: Sitka mountain ash, *S. sitchensis*, has rounded leaflets and ranges south to Oregon and Montana. Birds and animals feed on the berries in fall and winter.

Rose Family *(Rosaceae)*

BIRCHLEAF SPIRAEA

Spiraea betulifolia. Birchleaf spiraea reaches 10 to 20 inches tall and develops well-spaced colonies of plants from strong underground roots. A dense, flat-topped cluster of tiny white to pale pink flowers, that appear fuzzy from many protruding stamens, top the unbranched woody stems. The oval, alternate leaves, 1 to 2 inches long and toothed on the ends, resemble the leaves of birch trees. The blooms open in early to mid summer. HABITAT: Scattered to dense forest from low montane to subalpine altitudes. RANGE: Western Canada to Oregon and Wyoming and in Asia.

STEEPLEBUSH

Spiraea douglasii. This stunning shrub presents masses of tiny pink to brilliant rose flowers in elongated, pyramidal inflorescences. Shiny, oval leaves clothe the numerous branches that reach 2 to 6 feet high. Look for this beauty in the summer. HABITAT: It flourishes on stream banks and other wet or boggy sites from the coast to subalpine. RANGE: Idaho and peripheral areas of adjacent states, north to Alaska.

Rose Family *(Rosaceae)*

Rose Family *(Rosaceae)*

Madder Family *(Rubiaceae)*

PINK SPIRAEA, SUBALPINE SPIRAEA

Spiraea densiflora. These low shrubs, 2 to 4 feet high, create dazzling rose-pink floral displays. The individual flowers are tiny, about 1/8 inch long, but they form dense, flat-topped or rounded clusters, 1 to 3 inches across. They add a very pleasant fragrance to high mountain air. Many projecting stamens make them appear quite fuzzy. Bright green oval leaves with fine teeth on the upper half of the margins cover the many stems. The blossoms open in July. HABITAT: Subalpine stream banks, lake shores and alpine cirques. RANGE: British Columbia to Montana, Wyoming and California.

NORTHERN BEDSTRAW

Galium boreale. Northern bedstraw produces rounded masses of tiny, white or cream, four-petaled flowers on branch ends. The plants stand erect 8 to 30 inches tall. In cross section, the stems are square, a feature common to the mint family as well. Simple, narrow leaves attach in whorls of four at regular nodes along the stem. It blooms in summer. HABITAT: Variable from the seacoast to subalpine. RANGE: Much of the N hemisphere, south to California, Texas and West Virginia. COMMENT: In earlier times members of this family were used to fill mattresses. We have about a dozen species of *Galium* in our region, most of them inconspicuous and weedy.

Pitcher Plant Family *(Sarraceniaceae)*   Saxifrage Family *(Saxifragaceae)*

COBRA PLANT, CALIFORNIA PITCHER PLANT

Darlingtonia californica. Unique among the flowering plants of the Northwest, cobra plant sends up tubular, hooded leaves, 8 to 20 inches high, from creeping rhizomes. Two odd bracts or appendages that look like a moustache mask a hole under the lip of the hood. Nectar inside the leaf attracts flying insects into the hole, where downward-pointing, sticky hairs trap them. Enzymes in the exudate digest the insects and the plants absorb nitrogenous compounds from the insect juices for their own nutritional needs. These carnivorous, cobra-like leaves are mottled yellowish green, tinged with purple. The flowers with creamy sepals, 2 inches long, and shorter maroon petals, hang pendent from stems that may reach 3 feet in height. Blossoms can appear from April to August. HABITAT: Acid bogs and seeps or small streams. RANGE: Southwestern Oregon, from the coast into the mountains, and NW California to the Sierras.
COMMENT: Another carnivore, common butterwort, is described on p. 159.

GOOSEBERRY LEAVED ALUMROOT

Heuchera grossulariifolia. Leafless stems, 6 to 24 inches, erupt from a basal tuft of roundly heart-shaped leaves that are shallowly lobed numerous times. Cup-shaped or tubular flowers crowd the stem tip. Five tiny white petals perch on stalks from the base and expand (oar-shaped) at the tip. They peek out of the calyx cup, while five stamens hide within the cup. May to August. HABITAT: Lower elevation hillsides to rocky alpine slopes. RANGE: Western Montana to Oregon and Washington.

Saxifrage Family *(Saxifragaceae)*   Saxifrage Family *(Saxifragaceae)*

BULBOUS PRAIRIE STAR, WOODLAND STAR

Lithophragma bulbifera. The outstanding feature of this beguiling little plant is the numerous, tiny, red bulblets that replace many of the flowers, especially below the apex. It therefore reproduces itself both vegetatively and sexually. The purplish-tinted stems reach 2 to 10 inches tall and display a fine coating of gland-tipped hairs. The flowers normally show five white or pink petals that divide palmately into five narrow, pointed lobes, the middle lobe longer and wider than the laterals. A few blossoms make a raceme or occasionally a branching inflorescence. Palmately compound basal leaves, about 1 inch long, have three or five leaflets, while several stem leaves are three-lobed and the lobes three-parted. Look for the blooms in spring or early summer. HABITAT: Grassy prairies or deserts to open forests. RANGE: Southern British Columbia through the Great Basin and east to Alberta and Colorado.

SMOOTH PRAIRIE STAR

Lithophragma glabra. Smooth prairie star stands 4 to 12 inches high from a few basal leaves about 1 inch long. These leaves are palmately dissected into five main divisions that in turn have three irregular, rounded lobes. Usually two smaller leaves grow sessile and low on the stem. Sometimes they develop bulblets in leaf axils at the base of the plant. Purple, gland-tipped hairs on stems and leaves give the plants a pale, purplish cast. The terminal inflorescence normally has two to five flowers, crowded at first, but expanding later. Five white to pink petals are cut into three or five pointed lobes in springtime.
HABITAT: Grassy plains to open woods.
RANGE: Washington and N Oregon, east of the Cascades to W Montana.

Saxifrage Family *(Saxifragaceae)*

LEAFY MITREWORT, STARSHAPED MITREWORT

Mitella caulescens. Like perfect little snowflakes, five green or purplish petals of leafy mitrewort branch, about 1/8 inch long, into several pinnate, hair-like tentacles. These bewitching little petals attach to the rim of a small, green saucer, called a hypanthium, which sits in a cup formed by the five lobes of a calyx (the sepals). Five miniature stamens also rest on the surface of the hypanthium. This perennial normally lifts one floral stem 8 to 16 inches, the top half occupied by an open raceme of flowers that bloom from the top down, unique in this respect among *Mitellas* in the Northwest. One to three small stem leaves rest below the blooms and a few basal leaves attach with long petioles. The leaf blades spread five palmate lobes and numerous teeth on the edges. On close examination the plants possess many gland-tipped hairs. Spring is blooming time for this one. HABITAT: Streambanks and other wet places, woods and meadows. RANGE: British Columbia to Montana and NW California. COMMENT: *Mitella* has 12 species mostly native to W North America.

FRINGED GRASS OF PARNASSUS
Parnassia fimbriata. Prominent hair-like fringes decorate the narrowed petal bases of this sheer white, unmistakable and unforgettable charmer. Solitary saucer-shaped flowers about 1 inch in diameter terminate smooth, slender stems, 4 to 12 inches tall. Glossy green, heart-shaped or kidney-shaped leaves emerge from the base of the plant on relatively short petioles. One small, heart-shaped leaf clasps the stem at mid height as it blooms in summer. HABITAT: Common on mossy banks and other wet places from middle elevations to alpine. RANGE: Alaska to Alberta, California and New Mexico. COMMENT: One can find three other species of *Parnassia* in our region, but they lack the fringed petals that distinguish this one so markedly.

Saxifrage Family *(Saxifragaceae)*

Saxifrage Family *(Saxifragaceae)*

SPOTTED SAXIFRAGE
Saxifraga bronchialis. Beguiling spots of red, orange and yellow gloriously stipple five small white petals. The corolla of fused petals forms a shallow saucer that supports a superior white ovary and ten stamens. Numerous branching flower stems rise from leaf and stem tufts or cushions to 6 inches high. Needle-shaped leaves, 1/4 to 1/2 inch long, clothe the prostrate stems and may remain attached for several years. They bloom from late spring to midsummer. HABITAT: Rocky or gravelly sites, seashore to high alpine. RANGE: Circumpolar in the arctic, south to Oregon and New Mexico.

227

Saxifrage Family *(Saxifragaceae)*   Saxifrage Family *(Saxifragaceae)*

WESTERN SAXIFRAGE, REDWOOL SAXIFRAGE

Saxifraga occidentalis. Pyramidal or flat-topped heads of tiny, alluring flowers, white or pinkish, sit atop reddish, woolly stems. Typical of most saxifrages, the stems are leafless and mostly unbranched below the inflorescence. The leaves form a rosette at the base of the stem. They show many teeth on the edges and frequently reddish color on the under side. Flowers open early in the season, depending on elevation. HABITAT: Prairies, meadows or rocky outcrops, where moist in early spring but drying later. RANGE: Northwestern United States and SW Canada. COMMENT: More than 20 species of *Saxifraga* occur in our region. Western saxifrage has six poorly defined varieties. They often intergrade, one into another where ranges overlap, causing considerable variation in appearance within the species.

BUTTERCUP-LEAVED SUKSDORFIA

Suksdorfia ranunculifolia. Five white, oar-shaped petals rest on a shallow, cupped calyx and surround five yellow to purple or brownish stamens. Normally a single stem stands 4 to 12 inches tall and the inflorescence branches in a panicle. Most of the leaves originate from the base of the plant on unusually broad petioles. The leaf blades are pale green, succulent and rounded, but deeply cut into lobes and scalloped on the margins. Blooming can occur from May into August. HABITAT: Shallow soil on wet, mossy rocks from foothills to alpine. RANGE: British Columbia to California on the east slope of the Cascades to Alberta, Montana and NE Oregon.

Saxifrage Family *(Saxifragaceae)*

PURPLE SAXIFRAGE

Saxifraga oppositifolia. This dense cushion plant spreads many shrubby, prostrate branches up to 8 inches long. A single, glorious, purple or wine red flower tops each upright stem only 1 to 1 1/2 inches high. The rounded petals are about 1/4 to 3/8 inch long and create blossoms surprisingly large for the plants. Rounded leaves only about 1/8 inch long grow opposite on the stems and so tightly spaced that they overlap like shingles and may also show purplish tinges. Short, straight hairs line the leaf margins. Purple saxifrage blooms early in the alpine season. HABITAT: Rocky talus slopes, exposed ridges and rock outcrops above timberline. RANGE: Circumpolar in the arctic and south in high mountains to Washington, NE Oregon, Idaho and Wyoming.

Saxifrage Family *(Saxifragaceae)*

VIOLET SUKSDORFIA

Suksdorfia violacea. A more attractive species, violet suksdorfia has five somewhat unequal and irregularly spaced petals. From pale to deep violet, the few flowers on each plant make a branched inflorescence. One or more basal leaves are round or kidney-shaped, about 1 inch wide, have rounded lobes on the edge and often wither by blooming time in the spring. Three or more stem leaves grow smaller upward. From a swollen base that may develop bulblets, the slender stem reaches 4 to 10 inches high. HABITAT: Rocky places, shaded cliffs and mossy banks. RANGE: British Columbia to NW Montana and the Columbia Gorge.

FRINGECUP

Tellima grandiflora. Five petals, deeply cut or feathered, usually white or pink when first opened, turn dark red with age and fringe the lip of a green calyx cup. Many such blossoms make a raceme on one side of a stem 1 to 2 1/2 feet tall or more. Several stems sprout among a clump of long-stemmed, basal leaves, round or heart-shaped, 2 to 4 inches across, with shallow lobes and many irregular teeth on the edges. Leaf petioles and the lower flower stems carry a dense coat of coarse hairs. Spring and early summer for this one. HABITAT: Stream banks and moist woods. RANGE: Southern Alaska to central California, mostly west of the Cascade summit, but east across British Columbia to N Idaho.

Saxifrage Family *(Saxifragaceae)*

Saxifrage Family *(Saxifragaceae)*   **Saxifrage Family** *(Saxifragaceae)*

FOAMFLOWER, FALSE MITREWORT

Tiarella trifoliata var. *unifoliata*. An open
inflorescence of tiny, nodding flowers
decorate slender, branching stems. The
calyx and white petals create a shallow,
star-shaped cup filled with 10
prominently protruding, more or less
pendulous stamens. Maple-like leaves,
about 4 inches broad, grow on long
petioles from the base of the plant and
on short petioles on the flowering
stems. Look for these captivating little
charmers in early to mid summer.
HABITAT: Dense forest at medium
elevations. RANGE: Montana to
California and north to Alaska.
COMMENT: Trefoil foamflower has
three-lobed compound leaves, but
otherwise appears much the same.

YOUTH ON AGE

Tolmiea menziesii. Youth on age gets its
name from new leaf sprouts that start at
the base of old leaf blades. This unusual
habit can reproduce the plant
vegetatively. The flowers form a one-
sided raceme on hairy stems up to 2 or
even 3 feet long. Pretty, chocolate brown
calyx tubes, less than 1/2 inch long, split
on the under side almost to the base.
Four thread-like petals reflex and
enhance the beauty of the blooms.
Maple-like leaves, 2 to 8 inches long,
have irregular scallops on the margins.
This one may bloom from April to
August. HABITAT: It seeks moist forests
and stream banks at fairly low elevations.
RANGE: Southern Alaska to central
California from the western foothills of
the Cascades to the coast. COMMENT:
The genus *tolmiea* has only this one
species.

Figwort Family *(Scrophulariaceae)*

Figwort Family *(Scrophulariaceae)*

DESERT PAINTBRUSH

Castilleja chromosa. Desert paintbrush adds a touch of bright color to drab dryland terrain. The upper leaves and floral bracts, cut into three or five very narrow, spreading lobes, exhibit resplendent yellow, somewhat fluorescent orange or red hues. Clusters of unbranched stems grow 4 to 16 inches high. Lower leaves, 1 to 2 inches long, are usually simple. Stems, leaves and bracts all carry a fine pubescence. One can find desert paintbrush in bloom from April to August. HABITAT: Commonly on open plains, usually with sagebrush. RANGE: Eastern Oregon to central Wyoming and south to New Mexico and S California. COMMENT: Desert paintbrush has a look-alike in narrowleaf paintbrush, *C. angustifolia.* In all, the Northwest counts more than 40 species of Indian paintbrush in its spectacular flora.

HARSH PAINTBRUSH

Castilleja hispida. This paintbrush commonly erupts in a tuft of stems 8 to 24 inches tall. The lower leaves grow small and entire or simple, while the upper leaves below the inflorescence spread five or, more commonly, seven lobes. The lateral lobes are narrow and pointed and the central lobe broad and rounded. The bracts of the inflorescence usually have three or five lobes, similar in shape to the upper leaves. Dark red or scarlet or occasionally yellow hues color the floral bracts and some of the upper leaves. The inflorescence, compact at first, elongates later in the season. Rather coarse, sharply pointed hairs *(hispida)* generously coat the foliage. It blooms from mid spring to mid summer. HABITAT: Low to mid-elevation forest fringes and grassy openings. RANGE: Southern British Columbia and Alberta to NW Montana, S Idaho and SW Oregon.

SHOWY PAINTBRUSH

Castilleja pulchella. This Indian paintbrush normally sends up several stems from the base, not over 6 inches high. The upper leaves display a pair of wide-spreading, copiously hairy, lateral lobes. The bracts also split into three lobes, the central one rounded and laterals sharp-pointed. Yellow bracts as shown in the photo occur quite often, but reds and purples seem to predominate. It blooms in summer. HABITAT: Subalpine zone upward. RANGE: Montana, Wyoming and Utah. COMMENT: Many species of *Castilleja* hybridize readily, often making species identification very difficult.

Figwort Family *(Scrophulariaceae)*

Figwort Family *(Scrophulariaceae)*

CLIFF PAINTBRUSH

Castilleja rupicola. Delicate, almost lacy green leaves divide into three to seven narrow segments and several stems grow in a clump, 4 to 10 inches high. The bracts, which subtend the few flowers are parted like the leaves and tipped with pretty red or scarlet coloration. The green flowers hide behind the bracts at first, but continue to grow and later extend well into view. One can expect to find the blooms from spring into early summer. HABITAT: Wet cliffs and steep slopes from low elevation to subalpine. RANGE: The Cascades from S British Columbia to central Oregon.

Figwort Family *(Scrophulariaceae)*

Figwort Family *(Scrophulariaceae)*

STICKY BLUE EYED MARY

Collinsia rattanii. On simple or sparingly branched annual stems, often tinted purple, rest whorls of delicate little flowers in the axils of linear opposite leaves. The two-lipped blossoms are short, straight tubes that attach off center, making a sac at the base. Deep purple colors the lower lip, but two lobes of the upper lip contrast in white or lighter shades. Sticky, gland-tipped hairs more or less heavily beset the entire plant. *Rattan collinsia* blooms in spring. HABITAT: Open woods or brushy places. RANGE: Southwestern Washington to N California, west of the Cascades and in central Oregon. COMMENT: Three other species of *Collinsia* invest the Pacific Northwest, but they do not have the sticky hairs and their flower tubes bend noticeably.

FOXGLOVE

Digitalis purpurea. Many alien plants become weedy pests, but foxglove also adds ravishing beauty to the West Coast landscape. The heart stimulant, digitalis, comes from this source and it can be deadly poisonous to livestock when cured in hay. Numerous tubluar flowers, 1 1/2 to 2 1/2 inches long, droop from upright stalks 2 to 6 feet tall. Red or maroon to purple speckles adorn the lustrous white, pink to magenta blooms that usually decorate one side of the stem. Leaf size diminishes up the stem. It blooms from May to July. HABITAT: Roadsides and other disturbed ground to forest openings. RANGE: British Columbia to California, mainly west of the Cascades; orginally from Eurasia.

Figwort Family *(Scrophulariaceae)*

SCARLET MONKEYFLOWER

Mimulus cardinalis. Shocking splashes of scarlet rivet one's attention the instant this plant comes into view. Once seen in full bloom, scarlet monkeyflower will always be remembered. The blossom begins as a tube about 1 inch long and opens two lips about the same length. The upper lip, single-lobed, continues in line with the tube. Four lobes of the lower lip turn outward and down. Dark yellow marks the throat and white hairy stamens project straight out of the throat. The plants creep by rhizomes and rather lax stems reach 12 to 32 inches in length. Sticky, gland-tipped hairs cover stems, leaves and calyces. The sessile, opposite leaves have sharp teeth on the margins. Blooming can continue from spring into early fall. HABITAT: Wet, boggy places in the mountains. RANGE: South-western Oregon to Utah, Arizona and California.

Figwort Family *(Scrophulariaceae)*

Figwort Family *(Scrophulariaceae)*

CUSICK'S MONKEYFLOWER

Mimulus cusickii. These small plants grow in patches and sometimes produce gaudy splashes of color to enliven an otherwise drab landscape. Annual stems, 2 to 10 inches high, usually branch several times and bear rather sticky, gland-tipped hairs. The bright rose or magenta, tubular flowers rest in leaf axils. Typical of the genus, five petal lobes open wide into two lips, two above and three below. The hairy floral throat displays bright yellow and darker purple stripes or blotches. Oval or lance-shaped, opposite leaves taper to points and show prominent veins on the surface and entire (not lobed or toothed) margins. They bloom from mid spring through summer, responding especially well after a summer rain. HABITAT: Dry prairie or near desert. RANGE: Central Oregon and peripheral Idaho, Nevada and California. COMMENT: Bank monkeyflower, *M. clivicola* is a rare, smaller but similar annual that ranges from NE Oregon to N Idaho.

YELLOW MONKEYFLOWER

Mimulus guttatus. Yellow monkeyflower produces brilliant yellow tubes, 1/2 to 1 1/2 inches long that expand into two lips. Two ridges on the flaring lower lip tend to constrict the throat and display several reddish spots. Highly variable in growth habit, the plants reach 3 to 30 inches long and stand upright or recline. The luxuriant leaves are lance- or heart-shaped and sharply indented. Blooms from spring through summer. HABITAT: Moist soil and stream banks. RANGE: Western North America and introduced into many other parts of the world. COMMENT: One could easily mistake this for eight other species. Tooth-leaved monkeyflower, *M. dentatus*, prefers the coastal mountains, while alpine monkeyflower, *M. tilingii*, seeks out alpine heights.

Figwort Family *(Scrophulariaceae)*

LEWIS MONKEYFLOWER

Mimulus lewisii. This spectacular, pink to rose-red monkeyflower reaches about 1 1/2 inches in length. Within its five petal lobes nestles a yellow, hairy throat. Stems originate from creeping roots and grow 1 to 3 feet long, upright when short but tending to recline when long or uncrowded. They frequently form solid masses of growth in favorable locations. The opposite leaves are broadly lance-shaped, sticky hairy and indented on the margins. It blooms in summer. HABITAT: Wet stream banks and pool edges, subalpine and alpine. RANGE: British Columbia and Alberta to California and W Colorado. COMMENT: Named for Meriwether Lewis, this magnificent wildflower occurs quite commonly in its preferred habitat.

Figwort Family *(Scrophulariaceae)*

DWARF PURPLE MONKEYFLOWER

Mimulus nanus. On arid sites the entire plant may only reach 1 inch high, a single flower making up half the height. On better sites, well developed plants may branch profusely, reach 4 or 5 inches, and bear many crowded, 1-inch blossoms. The small but lustrous blooms, tubular and two-lipped, may vary from lavender to deep magenta or purple. Inside, two ridges on the lower lip carry bright yellow crests that contrast beautifully with darker purple spots. Soft, glandular or sticky hairs coat the simple elliptic leaves. The flowers may open from May into midsummer. HABITAT: Dry, sandy or gravelly soil from sagebrush prairies to piny woods in the mountains. RANGE: Central Washington to SW Montana, N California, Nevada and Yellowstone Park. COMMENT: Two other species of small magenta monkeyflowers inhabit the Great Basin.

Figwort Family *(Scrophulariaceae)*

TURTLEHEAD, WOODLAND BEARDTONGUE

Nothochelone nemorosa. Closely related to the penstemons, turtlehead blossoms comprise rather flattened tubes, 1 inch long or longer. They have a distinct ridge on top and two ridges on the lower lip within. Outside, the pink to magenta or purplish flowers wear a coat of short, gland-tipped hairs. Inside, woolly hairs cover four fertile anthers and one shorter, sterile stamen (staminode). The lower lip projects out much longer than the upper from a floral mouth about 1/2 inch wide. Several stems tend to sprawl, 12 to 32 inches long. Opposite, lance-shaped leaves all originate on the stems, those near the base much smaller than those above. The smooth, thin leaves show many strong, sharp teeth on the edges. Flowering occurs in summer. HABITAT: Woods to open rocky places, low elevation to near timberline. RANGE: Southwestern British Columbia to NW California, Cascades to the coast. COMMENT: *Nothochelone* has just one species.

Figwort Family *(Scrophulariaceae)*　　　　**Figwort Family** *(Scrophulariaceae)*

BUTTER AND EGGS

Triphysaria eriantha (Orthocarpus erianthus). Three small but gaudy sacs, the center one yellow and the others pearly white, make this little flower an eye-catcher. The sacs form the lower lip of a two-lipped blossom—the upper lip a sharp, purplish awl. A very slender hairy tube, 1/2 to 1 inch long, composes the floral base. Purple, fan-shaped bracts with mere filaments for lobes subtend the flowers. From the ground the plant usually branches into stems 2 to 14 inches long. Purple leaves 1/2 to 2 inches in length clasp the stem and spread two to four pairs of grasslike lobes. White, gland-tipped hairs give the plant a ghostly hue. It blooms in spring. HABITAT: Open, grassy areas along the coast. RANGE: Puget Sound to California. COMMENT: Recent taxonomic research dictates the scientific name changes shown above for both species on this page, from *Orthocarpus* to *Triphysaria* and *Castilleja* respectively.

HAIRY OWL CLOVER

Castilleja tenuis (Orthocarpus hispidus). This slender, hairy annual grows 4 to 16 inches high and bears all of its alternate leaves on one or a few stems. The lower, linear stem leaves broaden as they ascend the stem and become three- to five-lobed bracts that subtend the blossoms at the top. The tubular flowers, white or pale yellow, reach 1/2 to 3/4 inch long. Three lower petal lobes inflate into prominent sacs, while an upper petal forms a short upright beak, called a galea. Only the upper portion of the flower peeks out from behind its protective bract—from May into August. HABITAT: Meadows and other moist places. RANGE: Southern British Columbia to Idaho and S California.

Figwort Family *(Scrophulariaceae)*

Figwort Family *(Scrophulariaceae)*

BRACTED LOUSEWORT

Pedicularis bracteosa var. *bracteosa.*
Strange beauty characterizes these
flowers that form a dense spike or
raceme, subtended by narrow leafy
bracts that intermix with the blossoms.
Each yellow or reddish purple flower
has a narrow upper hood that may or
may not turn downward on the end into
a beak. The hood projects out over a
lower lip, composed of three fused
petals. Several unbranched stems, a
few inches to 3 feet tall, rise from the
root crown. The stems support
numerous alternate leaves, pinnately
lobed and sharply toothed, on short
petioles or sessile. The species may
also send up similar leaves from the
base on longer petioles or all of the
leaves may originate on the stems. It
blooms in summer. HABITAT: Moist soil
from mid montane to alpine. RANGE:
Western Canada to California and
Colorado. COMMENT: This variable
species sports no less than eight
varieties in the Northwest.

CANBY'S BRACTED LOUSEWORT

Pedicularis bracteosa var. *canbyi.* The
foliage of this variety of bracted
lousewort bears a sparse coating of long,
soft, cobwebby hairs. Dark purple stems
reach only about 3 to 5 inches high and
enchanting little flowers wear a delicate,
matchless shade of yellow. Opening from
the bottom upward, the blossoms are set
beautifully among dark purple, lance-
shaped bracts that shade to dark brown
if not black at the tip. Look for these
elegant little beauties in midsummer.
HABITAT: Alpine meadows and rocky
slopes. RANGE: Northern Idaho and W
Montana. COMMENT: Several species of
Pedicularis are semi-root parasites that
gain partial sustenance from other plants
through attachment of the roots.
Consequently, they cannot be
successfully transplanted.

Figwort Family (Scrophulariaceae)

FERNLEAF SICKLETOP, COILED LOUSEWORT

Pedicularis contorta. A fascinating upper petal coils downward, like a sickle above a broad lower lip. Many of these blossoms space themselves openly along the upper half of several slender stems, 6 to 24 inches high. Tiny teeth serrate the lobes of pinnately compound leaves, remindful of ferns. Most of the leaves sprout from the base on long petioles, but a few smaller leaves ascend the stems, becoming bracts in the inflorescence. It blooms from June into August. HABITAT: Moist meadows, woods and open, rocky slopes, most commonly subalpine and alpine. RANGE: Western Canada to N California and Wyoming. COMMENT: The common name, lousewort, apparently comes from an early superstition that lice populated the plants.

Figwort Family *(Scrophulariaceae)*

INDIAN WARRIOR

Pedicularis densiflorus. A dense spike of blood red, tubular and hooded flowers, 1 to 1 1/2 inches long, give this lousewort its common name. A rather inflated calyx encloses the base of each blossom and purplish, toothed bracts subtend the flowers. Several simple, hairy stems erupt from a strong taproot, surmounted by a dense tuft of basal leaves. These leaves are 3 to 8 inches long, purple tinged, pinnately lobed and toothed (fern-like). Stem leaves grow smaller but quite similar. It blooms from late winter to spring. HABITAT: Dry woods to 6000 feet elevation. RANGE: Southwestern Oregon to Baja.

Figwort Family *(Scrophulariaceae)*

Figwort Family *(Scrophulariaceae)*

ELEPHANTHEAD

Pedicularis groenlandica. These exquisite pink to magenta flowers unmistakably resemble elephants' heads. The upper petal, bulbous on top, imitates the animal's forehead and tapers into a long, narrow, gracefully curving trunk. Three lower petals spread wide to represent the ears and lower lip of the elephant. Many such flowers closely crowd the upper portions of unbranched stems. They stand 6 to 20 inches or more on reddish purple stems and bear the pinnately lobed, fernlike leaves common to the genus. One finds these amusing beauties in the summer. HABITAT: Frequents wet meadows at subalpine and alpine altitudes. RANGE: Transcontinental in Canada and south through the Cascades and Rockies. COMMENT: A smaller species occurs in the S Cascades and Sierras.

ALPINE DWARF LOUSEWORT

Pedicularis pulchella. On open alpine meadows and slopes dwells a charming lousewort so tiny that hikers can easily overlook it. The photographer must get down on his or her belly to focus on this one. The purple, two-lipped flower reaches less than 1 inch long, the upper lip forming a pronounced hood or short beak. Short, leaflike bracts subtend the blooms. Both leaves and bracts are deeply lobed and fern-like. It blooms in midsummer. HABITAT: Gravelly, rocky or mossy sites. RANGE: Western Montana and Wyoming.

Figwort Family *(Scrophulariaceae)*

PARRY'S PURPLE LOUSEWORT

Pedicularis parryi var. *purpurea*. This deep rose to magenta or purple lousewort rises 2 to 10 inches high in a spike or partial raceme. The parrot-beaked flowers curl modestly downward and end in a short beak. A three-lobed bract subtends each blossom, the margins lined with hairs. Most of the leaves sprout from the base. They are 2 to 4 inches long, narrow, deeply lobed pinnately, the margins of the pinnae marked with sharp teeth. Look for these captivating blooms in late spring and early summer. HABITAT: Scattered timber and open areas from medium to high altitudes. RANGE: Central Idaho, SW Montana, NW Wyoming and N Utah. COMMENT: The type variety, *parryi*, displays creamy flowers and occurs prominently in the alpine flora of the central and S Rockies.

Figwort Family *(Scrophulariaceae)*

Figwort Family *(Scrophulariaceae)*

SICKLETOP LOUSEWORT, PARROT'S BEAK

Pedicularis racemosa. Unlike our other louseworts, this one produces simple, lance-shaped leaves, toothed on the edges and frequently copper-toned. The leaves attach to a cluster of stems, 6 to 20 inches tall, on short petioles and readily differentiate this species from coiled lousewort, p. 242. Sickle-shaped upper petals curve gracefully over broad, three-lobed lower lips often few in number, the white, cream or pink flowers tend to crowd near the top of the stem. These flowers open in summer. HABITAT: Woods in the higher mountains, mostly subalpine. RANGE: Common throughout most of the West.

TAPER LEAVED PENSTEMON

Penstemon attenuatus. The specific Latin name, *attenuatus,* refers to the dark green, entire leaves of this impressive *Penstemon,* which taper to sharp, slender points, especially on the upper stem. The inflorescence is composed of two or more branching false whorls of flowers. Short, tubular blossoms, that can vary from cream to yellow to blue or purple, flare two lips, two-lobed above and three-lobed below, which is typical of most penstemons. Glandular hairs cover the upper leaves, stems and flowers, but the lower leaves are quite smooth. Several stems grow in a clump, 6 to 30 inches tall, from a woody, rhizomatous root. They bloom the first half of summer. HABITAT: Open prairies into the mountains. RANGE: Eastern Oregon and Washington to S Idaho, W Montana and Wyoming. COMMENT: Penstemon is the largest genus of plants native to North America, with approximately 270 species. Mostly found in the drier parts of the West, often on desert habitats. More than 50 species of *Penstemon* glorify our region. Many species adapt readily to flower gardens, especially if they do not receive too much tender loving care.

Figwort Family *(Scrophulariaceae)*

Figwort Family *(Scrophulariaceae)*

AZURE PENSTEMON

Penstemon azureus. A branching inflorescence that resembles whorls tends to decorate just one side of a flower stem. The deep blue to lilac or purple blooms begin as tubes about 1 inch long and flare widely to two lips. A glaucous coating often tints the blossoms outside. From a woody base the flower stems grow 8 to 20 inches tall. Entire, leathery leaves, 1 to 2 inches long, attach with short petioles at the base, while upper stem leaves grow smaller and clasp the stems. It blooms in late spring and early summer. HABITAT: Dry, open areas to forests and thickets in the mountains. RANGE: Southwestern Oregon into California. COMMENT: A very similar but smaller species, *P. parvulus,* occurs in the same range. Penstemon flowers normally have four fertile stamens and one sterile stamen. The sterile stamen is coated with hairs in many, but not all, species, giving rise to the common name "beard tongue".

HOTROCK PENSTEMON, SCORCHED PENSTEMON

Penstemon deustus. One of two white or yellowish species of penstemon in the Northwest, *deustus* sends up several unbranched, upright stems 4 to 24 inches. The mostly white or creamy flowers, 1/3 to 3/4 inches long, form several tight clusters along the upper stem and may show a tint of purple. Nearly sessile leaves, about 1 inch wide and 2 inches long, are lance shaped with small, sharp teeth on the edges. Hotrock penstemon blossoms from May into July. HABITAT: Dry, ordinarily rocky spots from low to high altitudes. RANGE: Central Washington to Montana and south to Utah and Nevada.

Figwort Family *(Scrophulariaceae)*

BARRETT'S PENSTEMON

Penstemon barrettiae. A raceme of rose- or lilac-colored, tubular flowers, 1 1/4 to 1 1/2 inches long, show a sharp ridge along the top of each blossom. Three petal lobes hang down in front and reveal a hairy palate within. Two lobes of the upper lip flare upward and allow one to see four white, woolly anthers inside. A shrubby base branches strongly and some branches are sterile, ie., do not bear flowers. The dark green, smooth, leathery leaves, about 3 inches long and 1 inch wide, may have toothed or entire margins. Flowers appear in spring. HABITAT: Inhabits rocky ledges or scree at lower elevations. RANGE: Endemic to the Columbia Gorge, around the eastern end.

Figwort Family *(Scrophulariaceae)*

Figwort Family *(Scrophulariaceae)*

SHRUBBY PENSTEMON

Penstemon fruticosus. This gorgeous wildflower has several large blue or lavender blossoms, 1 to 1 1/2 inches long, in a raceme that tends to attach on one side of the stem. White hairs impart a light fuzzy texture to the lower lip, which protrudes farther than the upper lip. The plant is a low shrub that may or may not spread and form ground-covering mats. Oval or linear, sharply indented or smooth-margined, the leaves vary according to the variety. Blossoms emerge from May to August, depending on elevation. HABITAT: Rocky or gravelly slopes in the mountains. RANGE: Oregon to Wyoming and north into Canada. COMMENT: We have three varieties of shrubby penstemon, which germinate readily from seed and often adapt quite easily to rock gardens.

GAIRDNER'S PENSTEMON

Penstemon gairdneri. Unusual for a *Penstemon*, this species has mostly alternate leaves. Also most of the leaves are linear and entire. Many stems, some of them without flowers, rise 4 to 16 inches from a woody root crown and often create loose mats. The flowers also alternate in a raceme or make few flowered whorls. The dark red to purplish flowers reach 2/3 to nearly 1 inch long and grow hairs both inside and out. A hairy beard tips the sterile stamen, but the fertile anthers are hairless. This one blooms in May and June. HABITAT: Dry rocky places with thin soil from valleys into the mountains. RANGE: Central and E Washington, E Oregon and SW Idaho.

Figwort Family *(Scrophulariaceae)*

PAYETTE PENSTEMON

Penstemon payettensis. These robust, nearly hairless plants have up to six or more closely stacked, false whorls of large, lustrous blue flowers tinted with lavender. Individual blossoms measure 3/4 to 1 1/4 inch long, truly a magnificent sight. The floral tubes open about 1/2 inch wide at the mouth to reveal hairless anthers that are somewhat S-shaped. Several strong stems reach 8 to 28 inches tall from a thick basal rosette of bright green leaves, which are about 6 inches long. As the upper leaves scale the stems, they grow smaller, sessile and even clasp the stem near the top. Look for these matchless beauties from May to August, depending upon altitude. HABITAT: Open meadows and slopes with good drainage, valleys to ridge tops. RANGE: Southern Idaho and adjacent Blue Mountains of Oregon.

Figwort Family *(Scrophulariaceae)*

Figwort Family *(Scrophulariaceae)*

SMALL FLOWERED PENSTEMON, CLUSTERED PENSTEMON

Penstemon procerus. Several stems grow in a tuft and one or more dense clusters of small, intense blue or sometimes cream-colored flowers terminate the stems. The clusters appear as whorls, but actually grow on short peduncles, originating in leaf axils. Several pairs of opposite leaves, bright green, entire and sessile decorate the stems. Some larger, lance-shaped leaves on petioles may garnish the base of the plant. Look for these engaging beauties in early summer. HABITAT: Well-drained slopes and meadows in the mountains. RANGE: Northern Canada and Alaska to Colorado and California. COMMENT: Rydberg's penstemon closely resembles this one.

ROCK (CLIFF) PENSTEMON

Penstemon rupicola. Startling rose-red to fuschia flowers, 1 to 1 1/2 inches long, sometimes literally cover a low cushion plant, making brilliant splashes of color against bare rock. Each rather slender flower has a marked ridge on top and woolly hairy anthers within. From a shrubby, matted base the plant sends up many flowering stems to 4 inches long, each bearing a few-flowered raceme at the top. The woody branches carry small, 1/3 to 2/3 inch, toothed leaves, round or oval, quite leathery and wearing bluish, glaucous coats. The leaves on the flower stems grow smaller and become mere bracts at the top. Blooms from late spring to midsummer, depending on elevation. HABITAT: Cliffs and rock outcrops from low elevation to near timberline. RANGE: The Cascades of Washington to the Siskiyous of NW California.

Figwort Family *(Scrophulariaceae)*

ROYAL PENSTEMON

Penstemon speciosus. One of the more robust penstemons in the Northwest, royal penstemon can reach 3 feet tall. Numerous false whorls of gaudy blue flowers embellish the plants and may tend to grow on one side of the stem. S-shaped anthers show in the throats of the 1 to 1 2/3 inch flowers. Basal leaves to 6 inches long form a rosette. They are slender, widening near the end and tapering to a relatively long petiole. Narrow or linear stem leaves attach without petioles, sessile to clasping. Search for these fantastic blossoms from May to July. HABITAT: Dry, open terrain, prairies to scattered forest. RANGE: The Columbia Basin and Great Basin, central Washington to S Idaho, E Utah and California.

Figgwort Family *(Scrophulariaceae)*

Figgwort Family *(Scrophulariaccae)*

CASCADE PENSTEMON

Penstemon serrulatus. Cascade penstemon commonly produces a single large terminal cluster of dark blue to lavender or purple flowers, but sometimes false whorls (branching peduncles) appear on the stems as well. The individual blossoms reach 2/3 to 1 inch long, have horseshoe-shaped anthers and a yellow beard on the sterile stamen. The 1- to 3-inch, sharply toothed leaves all attach opposite and mostly sessile on the stems, the lower ones smaller than those above. Several to many stems grow 8 to 28 inches tall and bloom in summer. HABITAT: Wet ground, open or forested to quite high in the mountains. RANGE: The Cascades to the coast, S British Columbia to Oregon.

YELLOW RATTLE, RATTLE BOX

Rhinanthus christa-galli. A unique little yellow blossom peeks out of an inflated pale green calyx, about 1/2 inch long, that projects four sharp-pointed lobes. The upper floral hood is very short and shows two small, often white lobes on the sides. The lower lip has three small lobes. This plant displays a spike of such flowers that sprout from the axils of upper leaf-like bracts. The pale green, lance-shaped leaves, 1 to 2 1/2 inches long, have sharp teeth and grow opposite and sessile. It blooms in summer. HABITAT: Open fields and slopes to subalpine elevations. RANGE: The N hemisphere, south to N Oregon, Colorado and New York.

Figwort Family *(Scrophulariaceae)*

MOUNTAIN KITTENTAIL

Synthyris missurica. A regal blue or lavender raceme of tiny, cup-shaped flowers ascends four to 20 inches high. The 4 petals are unequal in size—the upper somewhat larger than the others. Two purple stamens and one pistil from each blossom make the inflorescence fairly bristle. A rosette of round or kidney-shaped basal leaves on long petioles, 1 to 3 inches across, show rounded lobes or teeth on the margins. They bloom early in the season depending upon elevation. HABITAT: A plant of moist shady forests. RANGE: Northern Idaho and W Montana to the Blue Mountains and NE California.

SNOW QUEEN

Synthyris reniformis. A tuft of flower stems and leaves erupt from a root crown. The broadly oval or kidney-shaped leaves, 1 to 3 inches across, rest on long petioles and have scalloped edges. Slender, weak flower stems grow shorter than the leaves, 2 to 6 inches. A rather sparsely flowered raceme of purple to sometimes white (mostly lilac), cup-shaped flowers crown the stems from February to April or May. HABITAT: A lower elevation forest sprite. RANGE: Washington to California, west of the Cascades, except for the Columbia Gorge.

Figwort Family *(Scrophulariaceae)*

Figgwort Family *(Scrophulariaceae)*

COLUMBIA KITTENTAILS

Synthyris stellata. Tightly clustered racemes of sky blue to cobalt flowers, about 1/4 inch long, flourish atop succulent stems, 4 to 12 inches long. Each blossom features four rounded petals, cupped or somewhat spreading, two stamens and one projecting style. The plants spread by rhizomes and create crowded colonies on favorable sites. Most of the leaves spring from the base on long petioles. The round, shiny green leaf blades tend to form cups or shallow funnels and effect many sharp teeth in a regular, alternating, deep-shallow pattern on the rims. A few reduced stem leaves become small, lance-shaped bracts in the inflorescence. Search for this one in spring. HABITAT: Wet mossy rocks and slopes, usually north facing or deeply shaded. RANGE: Endemic to the Columbia Gorge.

Figwort Family *(Scrophulariaceae)*

Figwort Family *(Scrophulariaceae)*

BEAUTIFUL TONELLA

Tonella floribunda. Both the flowers and leaves of this cheerful, showy little annual or biennial attach in whorls at regular nodes along the upper stems. From short tubes the numerous blossoms flare five white or pale lavender petal lobes. Dark purple veins gloriously mark the upper petals, while gland-tipped hairs cover the peduncles. The upper leaves are quite narrow, simple and sessile, but the lower stem leaves have broader, three-parted lobes on moderate length petioles.

Depauperate plants on very shallow soil may develop simple stems, but on better sites the plants branch profusely. They bloom in spring. HABITAT: Open rocky slopes and bunchgrass foothills and canyons. RANGE: Limited to the Blue Mountains of E Oregon and Washington and adjacent Idaho, mainly in the Snake River canyon.

CUSICK'S SPEEDWELL or BROOKLIME

Veronica cusickii. Underground rhizomes send up single stems, 2 to 8 inches, at regularly spaced nodes. Smooth, shiny-green, succulent leaves, 1/2 to 1 inch long, sit opposite on the stems and expand widest in the middle. A tight raceme of deep blue to violet flowers about 3/8 to 1/2 inch broad, show darker parallel veins. A white eye may or may not mark the floral center. A single style about 1/4 inch long curves gracefully out beyond two shorter stamens to distinguish this species. The upper petal is widest and the lower the smallest of the four petals, typical of the genus *Veronica.* The flowers bloom in sequence from the bottom upward and gland-tipped hairs mark the inflorescence and sometimes the upper leaves, appearing as white spots in the photo. Short, threadlike peduncles support the blossoms in July and August. HABITAT: Moist alpine and subalpine heights. RANGE: Southern British Columbia to W Montana, NE Oregon and the Sierras.

Valerian Family *(Valerianaceae)*

Valerian Family *(Valerianaceae)*

ROSY PLECTRITIS, SEA BLUSH

Plectritis congesta. Round balls of bright pink, or occasionally white, flowers terminate a simple or few-branched annual stem, 4 to 18 inches high. Entire hillsides or fields sometimes blaze with the joyous spring bloom. The individual flower is a tiny, five-lobed tube that produces a very short spur at the base. The spur goes unnoticed without magnification. Widely spaced pairs of opposite leaves reach 1/2 to 2 inches in length, grow club-shaped near the base and elliptic and sessile above. HABITAT: Open moist ground that dries by summer. RANGE: From the coast to the Cascades, S Vancouver Island to S California. COMMENT: We also have two very similar species with much longer, noticeable spurs, one with mostly white flowers.

EDIBLE VALERIAN, TOBACCO ROOT

Valeriana edulis. From a thick edible taproot comes a tuft of basal leaves, 3 to 16 inches long and mostly narrow and simple. A single erect stem rises 4 to 48 inches and carries up to six pairs of opposite leaves cut into narrow pinnate lobes. The plant branches in the inflorescence, a panicle, with a multitude of tiny flowers compactly clustered at the peak of blooming. The inflorescence expands later. The flowers are yellowish white, sometimes with a pink blush, in summer. HABITAT: Usually wet, open meadows or bogs, but also on drier sites into the mountains. RANGE: Southern British Columbia, east of the Cascades, to S Mexico and sporadic east to Ontario and Ohio.

SITKA VALERIAN, MOUNTAIN HELIOTROPE

Valeriana sitchensis. Small, white, funnel-shaped flowers, pinkish in the bud, crowd into rounded or hemispheric floral heads, 1 to 3 inches across. Five fused petals form the corolla tube and many stamens protrude from these arresting blossoms. Two or more pairs of opposite leaves attach mostly on the flower stems. They are pinnately compound, usually with three or five oval or lance-shaped leaflets, the terminal leaflet the largest. Coarse shallow teeth mark the leaflet margins. The plants typically stand 1 to 3 feet tall and bloom from June to August. HABITAT: Moist ground on wooded slopes or meadows from mid montane to alpine. RANGE: Alaska to Montana and California. COMMENT: About seven valerians, separable on technical characters, inhabit the Northwest.

Valerian Family *(Valerianaceae)*

Violet Family *(Violaceae)*

EARLY BLUE VIOLET

Viola adunca. These lovely blue violets commonly grow in low clumps, the flower stems branching from a central stem that may be very short and indistinct. Showy white beards and dark purple guide lines usually mark the lower three petals. The lowest petal projects backward into a short curved spur. The leaves, mostly basal, are heart-shaped. A spring to midsummer bloomer. HABITAT: Moist woods and meadows. RANGE: Most of North America.

Violet Family*(Violaceae)*

Violet Family*(Violaceae)*

BECKWITH'S VIOLET

Viola beckwithii. Beckwith's violet is one of four species of *Viola* in the Northwest that have multicolored flowers and deeply cut leaves. Its lustrous blooms feature two very dark, reddish purple, upper petals and three pale-colored or white lower petals, a yellow throat and purple guide lines on the lower petals. Guide lines are thought to lead bees and other pollinating insects to nectar in the sac created by a backward projection of the bottom petal. All leaves and flower stems originate on a root crown below ground and thus create a tufted plant. The stems reach 2 to 5 inches high. Leaf blades are pinnately compound and the primary segments further develop three or five narrow lobes. They bloom early, from March to May. HABITAT: Sagebrush prairies and foothills to piny woods. RANGE: Eastern Oregon and Idaho to Utah and E California.

STREAM VIOLET

Viola glabella. Several attractive, yellow violets, about 1/2 inch long, perch on smooth slender stems. The floral stem branches only near the top and flowers grow from upper leaf axils. The blossoms beckon flying insects with pretty purple guide lines on the lower three petals and little white beards on the lateral two. Glossy green leaves are broadly heart-shaped with small sharp teeth on the edges. The leaves generally taper to sharp points at the tip. They bloom in spring and early summer. HABITAT: Stream banks and wet woods. RANGE: Asia and Alaska to California and Montana.

Violet Family *(Violaceae)*

MACLOSKEY'S (SMALL WHITE) VIOLET

Viola macloskeyi. These admirable white violets possess two upright, rounded petals above, two on the sides that arch downward and a broad lower lip petal, distinctly indented on the end. The two lateral petals disclose small white beards near the base and purple veins mark the three lower petals. Solitary flowers crown slender peduncles 1 1/2 to 3 1/2 inches tall, that originate at the root crown. Heart- or lance-shaped leaves also rise from the root, lower than the flowers and reveal small rounded teeth on the margins. Blooming occurs early in the season. HABITAT: Wet, soggy ground, canyon bottoms to mountains. RANGE: Much of North America, north of Mexico.

Selected References

1. Booth, W. E. and J. C. Wright. 1959. *Flora of Montana, Part II*. Montana State Univ. Bozeman.

2. Chambers, K. L. 1992. Some Recent Taxonomic Changes Affecting the Names of Oregon Plant Species. *Kalmiopsis*. Vol. 2.

3. Clark, L. J. 1976. *Wild Flowers of the Pacific Northwest*. Gray's. Sidney, B. C.

4. Cormack, R.G.H. 1977.*Wildflowers of Alberta*. Hurtig. Edmonton.

5. Craighead, J. J., F. C. Craighead and R. J. Davis. 1963. *A Field Guide to Rocky Mountain Wildflowers*. Houghton Mifflin. Cambridge.

6. Dorn, R. D. 1984. *Vascular Plants of Montana*. Mountain West. Cheyenne.

7. Eastman, D. C. 1990. *Rare and Endangered Plants of Oregon*. Beautiful America. Wilsonville, OR.

8. Hitchcock, C. L. and A. Cronquist. 1973. *Flora of the Pacific Northwest*. Univ of Wash. Seattle.

9. Hitchcock, C. L. and A. Cronquist, M. Ownbey and J. W. Thompson, eds. 1955 to 1969. *Vascular Plants of the Pacific Northwest*, in 5 vols. Univ. of Wash. Seattle.

10. Jolley, R. 1988. *Wildflowers of the Columbia Gorge*. Oregon Hist. Soc. Portland.

11. Larrison, E. J., G. W. Patrick, W. H. Baker and J. A. Yaich. 1974. *Washington Wildflowers*. Audubon Soc. Seattle.

12. Lesica, P. 1985. *Checklist of Vascular Plants of Glacier National Park*. Montana Ac. of Sci.

13. Lodewick, K. and R. 1970. *Penstemon Field Identifier, Part I*. Eugene.

14. Lyons, C. P. 1956. *Trees, Shrubs and Flowers to Know in Washington*. Evergreen. Vancouver.

15. Moss, E. H. 1959. *Flora of Alberta*. Univ. of Toronto.

16. Munz, P. and D. Keck. 1959. *A California Flora*. Univ. of Calif. Berkeley.

17. Niehaus, T. F. and C. L. Ripper. 1976. *A Field Guide to Pacific States Wildflowers*. Houghton Mifflin. Boston.

18. Orr, R. T. and M. C. 1981. *Wildflowers of Western America*. Galahad. N. Y.

19. Patterson, P. A., K. Neiman and J. Tonn. 1985. *Field Guide to Forest Plants of Northern Idaho*. USDA For. Ser.

20. Peck, M. E. 1961. *Manual of the Higher Plants of Oregon*. Binford and Morts. Portland.

21. Rickett, H. W. 1973. *Wildflowers of the United States, Vol. 6, The Central Mountains and Plains*. McGraw Hill. NY.

22. Ross, R. A. and H. L. Chambers. 1988. *Wildflowers of the Western Cascades*. Timber Press. Portland.

23. Shaw, R. J. and D. On. 1979. *Plants of Waterton-Glacier National Parks*. Mountain Press. Missoula.

24. Scotter, G. W. and H. Flygare. 1986. *Wildflowers of the Canadian Rockies*. Hurtig. Edmonton.

25. Spellenberg, R. 1979. *Audubon Society Field Guide to North American Wildflowers, Western Region*. Knopf. N. Y.

26. Standley, P. C. 1921. *Flora of Glacier National Park, Montana*. GPO. Wash.

27. St. John, H. 1963. *Flora of Southeastern Washington*. Edwards Bros.

28. Strickler, D. 1986. *Prairie Wildflowers*. Flower Press. Columbia Falls, MT.

29. _____. 1988. *Forest Wildflowers*. Flower Press. Columbia Falls, MT.

30. _____. 1990. *Alpine Wildflowers*. Flower Press. Columbia Falls, MT.

Illustrated Glossary

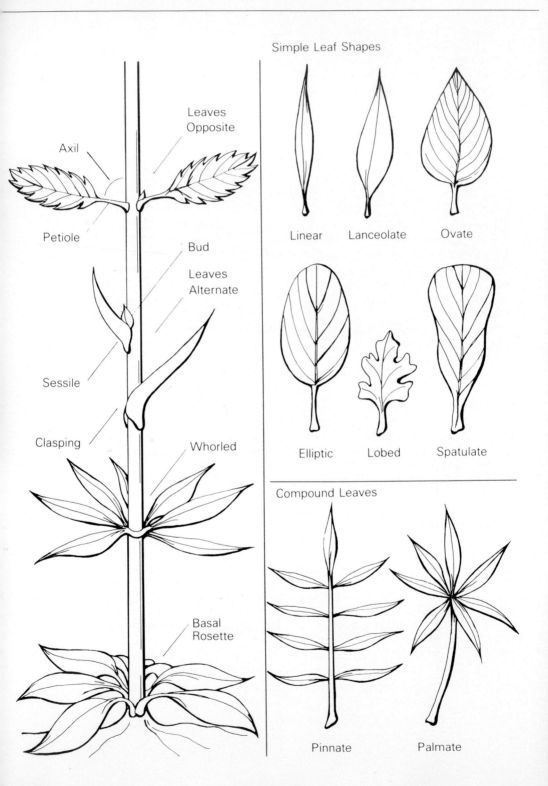

Simple Leaf Shapes

Linear   Lanceolate   Ovate

Elliptic   Lobed   Spatulate

Leaves Opposite

Axil

Petiole

Bud

Leaves Alternate

Sessile

Clasping   Whorled

Basal Rosette

Compound Leaves

Pinnate   Palmate

Glossary

Annual — A plant that completes its life cycle in one year.
Anther — The pollen-producing appendage on the stamen.
Banner — The uppermost petal of a pea flower.
Berry — A fleshy fruit, usually juicy, containing one or more seeds.
Biennial — A plant living for part or all of two years before dying.
Blade — The broad part of a leaf.
Bract — A leaf-like scale on a flower or flower cluster.
Bulb — A plant bud usually below ground.
Calyx — The outermost portion of a flower, the sepals collectively.
Catkin — A dense spike or raceme with many scales and small naked flowers.
Clasping — As a leaf base surrounding a stem.
Column — A group of united stamens and pistils.
Compound leaf — Composed of two or more leaflets.
Corm — A bulb-like but solid underground swelling of a stem.
Corolla — Collectively the petals of a flower.
Disc flower or floret — Tubular flowers at the center of a composite head.
Drupe — A fleshy fruit with a stone-encased seed.
Entire — As a leaf margin, not toothed, lobed or cut.
Gland — A spot or expanded area that produces a sticky substance.
Glaucous — Fine powder coating a surface.
Head — A cluster of flowers crowding the tip of a stem.
Hybrid — Pollination of a plant by another species or variety.
Inflorescence — An arrangement of flowers on a stem.
Irregular — Nonsymmetrical in shape or orientation.
Nectar — A sweet liquid produced by flowers that attracts insects.
Node — A point on a stem where leaves or branches originate.
Ovary — Part of the pistil containing the developing seeds.
Pedicel — The supporting stem of a single flower.
Peduncle — The stalk of an inflorescence or a single flower.
Perennial — A plant that lives more than two years.
Petals — The floral leaves, often colored, inside the sepals.
Petiole — The stem supporting a leaf.
Pistil — The female organ of a flower—stigma, style and ovary combined.
Pollen — Masculine cells produced by the stamens.
Raceme — An inflorescence on a single stalk composed of flowers on pedicels.
Ray flowers or florets — Strap-shaped flowers in a composite head.
Rhizome — A horizontal underground stem or rootstock.
Saprophyte — A plant that lives on dead, decayed organic matter.
Sepal — Outermost floral leaf, one segment of the calyx.
Serrate — Having short sharp teeth on the margin.
Sessile — Attached at the base, lacking a stem or pedicel.
Sheathed — Enclosing a stem at the base, clasping.
Shrub — A woody plant smaller than a tree.
Spathe — A large bract subtending or enclosing an inflorescence.
Spike — An inflorescence of sessile flowers on a single stalk.
Spur — A hollow appendage of a petal or sepal.
Stamen — The pollen producing organ of a flower.
Stigma — The end of the pistil that collects pollen.
Stolon — A horizontal stem from the base of a plant.
Style — The slender stalk of a pistil.
Succulent — Pulpy, soft and juicy.
Tendril — A slender twining extension of a leaf or stem.
Tepals — Undifferentiated sepals and petals collectively.
Umbel — A group of stems or pedicels that arise from a common point on a stalk.
Whorl — Three or more leaves or branches growing from a node or common point.

Index

Index

Index

Index

Index

Back Cover: Sunflower Family *(Asteraceae, Compositae)*

HOOKER'S THISTLE

Cirsium hookerianum. Hooker's thistle sends up a stem 16 to 60 inches tall that may branch sparingly but often does not. The stem tapers, unlike elk thistle, but because the two species tend to hybridize, the taper may not be strongly noticeable, especially in the southern part of its range. White, woolly hairs also dress the stems. Creamy flower heads tend to crowd the stem tips, and a few smaller heads may scatter below the crown in leaf axils. The bracts of the floral heads bear sharp, short spines. The leaves are typically quite narrow, shallowly lobed and the lobes spine-tipped. Blooming occurs in summer. HABITAT: Open rocky slopes and meadows from valleys to lower alpine. RANGE: British Columbia and Alberta to N Washington and Montana, east of the cascades.

The author, Dee Strickler, prepares to photograph **HOOKER'S THISTLE,** *Cirsium hookerianum,* in one of his favorite wildflower haunts, Glacier National Park. Cracker Lake in the background rests at the base of Siyeh Peak as summer thunderheads build over the mountain.